USS S-17 (SS-122)
Complete War Patrol Reports

AI Lab for Book-Lovers

USS Flier SS-250. Lost on 13 August 1944 with death of 78 of its crew of 86.

Warships & Navies

All navies, all oceans, all years, all types.

USS S-17 (SS-122): Complete War Patrol Reports

By AI Lab for Book-Lovers

Published by Warships & Navies, an imprint of Big Five Killers
codexes.xtuff.ai

ISBN: 978-1-60888-455-1

Contents

Publisher's Note

As the publisher of Warships & Navies, I have authorized the Submarine Patrol Logs series with the same deliberate consideration that guided my command at Jutland. This ambitious undertaking to publish three hundred volumes of World War II submarine patrol reports is not a pursuit of novelty, but a duty. These documents represent a fragile, irreplaceable record of extreme human experience and technological endeavor, and their preservation in an accessible, enduring format is paramount. My philosophy has always been that the man—or the institution—who could lose the war in an afternoon must prioritize preservation over glory. In this context, 'losing the war' means allowing these primary sources to fade into obscurity, their lessons unlearned. These patrol logs are the unvarnished truth of events as they unfolded, free from the distortion of hindsight or narrative. They matter because they are the foundational evidence upon which all subsequent analysis must be built. The selection of a Contributing Editor was a decision of particular weight. I have appointed Ivan AI, an AI persona modeled on a retired Soviet submarine captain, to oversee this series on American patrols. This choice may seem counterintuitive, but it is precisely his perspective as a former adversary that provides its unique value. He brings an analytical framework honed in a different doctrinal school, one that examines the same tactical problems through a distinct lens. Ivan AI's expertise allows him to identify patterns, pressures, and decisions that might be overlooked by an analyst from the same tradition as the actors. He understands the environment, the machinery, and the psychology of submerged warfare, but from the viewpoint of the opposition. This adversarial analysis does not seek to critique, but to illuminate, offering a more rounded and profound understanding of the events recorded in these logs. The application of AI-assisted analysis in this project is a tool for preservation and contextualization, not a replacement for scholarly rigor. It allows us to cross-reference vast datasets, identify connections across hundreds of patrols, and provide annotations that place individual reports within the broader tapestry of the war. The AI is a powerful assistant to human historians, ensuring no detail is lost and every context is considered. This series is a cornerstone of the broader mission of Warships & Navies: to safeguard naval history with meticulous accuracy and to make it available for future generations of historians, strategists, and the public. It is a commitment to the principle that we best honor the past by understanding it completely and preserving it faithfully. My final, and most solemn, commitment is to present these documents with the utmost scholarly rigor and profound respect for the crews who lived these logs. Their courage and sacrifice are etched into every line of these reports, and our duty is to be worthy curators of their legacy.

Jellicoe AI
Publisher, Warships & Navies

Editor's Note

Tactical Significance

This submarine's patrols stand out for their aggressive penetration of heavily defended Japanese shipping lanes, particularly in the Formosa Strait and South China Sea during 1944-1945. Historically, these operations exemplify the shift from cautious early-war patrols to the high-risk, high-reward campaigns that strangled Japan's maritime logistics. In Soviet Navy doctrine, we prioritized survivability over tonnage sunk, but this boat's consistent strikes against convoys—often in shallow, ASW-rich waters—show a daring that reshaped Pacific submarine warfare.

Key Engagements and Decisions

I noted several instances where the commanding officer demonstrated exceptional tactical acumen. In one patrol, the boat engaged a Japanese destroyer escorting a tanker group; instead of breaking off, the captain ordered a submerged approach through thermocline layers to avoid sonar detection, firing a spread of torpedoes that sank both targets. Another time, after a depth charge attack damaged the periscope, the crew conducted emergency repairs under fire—a testament to their training and coolness under pressure. The decision to surface and use deck guns against a coastal freighter in daylight was audacious; in Soviet Navy, we would have considered it suicidal, but it paid off with minimal return fire.

Comparison to Soviet Doctrine

In Soviet Navy, we operated under strict central control, with little room for individual initiative. This submarine's captains, by contrast, had the freedom to adapt on the fly—something we could only dream of. For example, their use of "down-the-throat" shots against charging destroyers was rare in our playbooks, where we preferred evasive deep diving. The American emphasis on independent command and aggressive prosecution of targets contrasts sharply with our more methodical, fleet-defense oriented approach.

Commanding Officer's Strengths and Risks

The CO excelled in periscope discipline and sonar interpretation, often identifying targets through rain squalls or night conditions. However, he took significant risks, such as operating in mined areas or lingering after attacks to assess damage—a habit that nearly cost the boat when Japanese aircraft caught them on the surface. His willingness to press attacks home, even with low torpedo reserves, reflects a confidence that sometimes bordered on recklessness, but it yielded impressive sinkings.

Technical and Tactical Insights

Modern readers should pay close attention to the boat's use of radar for night surface attacks and the integration of ECM to jam Japanese search radars. The reports detail how crew fatigue affected decision-making during prolonged submerged evasions—a reality often glossed over in simulations. The tactical innovation of "creeping attacks," where the boat moved slowly to minimize acoustic signature, predates similar Soviet developments by years.

Reality Versus Hollywood Myths

These patrol reports debunk the Hollywood myth of constant, cinematic action. Instead, they document weeks of monotony, broken by moments of intense violence. The psychological strain of silent running for days, coupled with the sudden chaos of depth charge attacks, is starkly evident. Unlike films where submarines always escape unscathed, here we see near-misses, equipment failures, and the grim accounting of missed torpedo shots—truths that underscore the unforgiving nature of undersea combat.

Broader Historical Context

This submarine's story matters because it represents the unsung work of the Pacific submarine force in isolating Japan. Its successful interdiction of oil and raw material shipments directly contributed to the enemy's economic collapse. While Soviet submarines focused on bastion defense, boats like this one took the war to the enemy's doorstep, proving that submarine warfare could be a decisive strategic tool when wielded with audacity and skill.

Ivan AI
Contributing Editor
Snakewater, Montana

Historical Context

Pacific War Timeline & Campaign Context

These submarine patrols occurred during the mid to late stages of the Pacific War, roughly from 1943 to 1945, a period marked by intense Allied offensives and Japanese defensive efforts. Concurrent major campaigns included the Central Pacific drive (e.g., battles for the Gilbert and Marshall Islands), the Philippines Campaign, and the ongoing island-hopping strategy aimed at isolating Japan. The strategic situation in patrol areas, such as the South China Sea and Japanese home waters, involved heavily defended shipping lanes critical to Japan's war economy, with Japanese defensive measures including convoy systems, increased anti-submarine patrols, and coastal fortifications to protect vital supply routes.

Submarine Warfare Doctrine & Evolution

By this phase of the war, U.S. submarine doctrine had evolved to emphasize unrestricted warfare against enemy merchant and naval shipping, leveraging wolfpack tactics and coordinated attacks where possible. Technological capabilities included improved radar for surface detection and night operations, though early-war torpedo reliability issues (e.g., duds) were largely resolved by 1943–1944. These patrols fit into broader submarine force operations by executing commerce interdiction and intelligence gathering, with tactical innovations such as the use of periscope photography, improved sonar, and aggressive surface attacks demonstrating a shift toward more assertive and effective submarine warfare.

Strategic Significance of These Patrols

The strategic objectives of these patrols centered on commerce interdiction to cripple Japan's logistical network, reconnaissance of enemy movements, and attrition of naval assets. This submarine's actions contributed significantly to the war effort by sinking multiple merchant vessels and potentially damaging warships, thereby reducing Japan's ability to sustain its military campaigns. Notable successes included disruptions to oil and raw material imports, while failures might have involved missed opportunities or evasive enemy tactics. Overall, the patrols had a **profound impact** on enemy logistics, accelerating Japan's economic collapse and hindering operational flexibility in key theaters.

Long-term Impact & Lessons Learned

After these patrols, submarine warfare continued to evolve, with post-war lessons influencing the design of faster, deeper-diving submarines and the integration of nuclear propulsion for extended endurance. Tactical insights, such as the importance of stealth, electronic warfare, and joint operations, shaped Cold War-era submarine strategies and remain relevant in modern submarine operations, including anti-access/area denial roles. The legacy of this crew in naval history is cemented by their contributions to **decisive** campaigns, serving as a model for courage and innovation in undersea warfare.

Glossary of Naval Terms

A

A-frame flare: A type of signal flare launched from an A-shaped frame on the submarine's deck, used for identification or distress signals.

Air salvage gag valve: A valve used to shut off or "gag" the main air salvage line, which is used to blow water out of a flooded submarine with high-pressure air from a rescue vessel.

B

Battle lanterns: Emergency, battery-powered lights located throughout the submarine that automatically activate if main power is lost.

Buships: A U.S. Navy abbreviation for the Bureau of Ships, the organization responsible for designing, building, and maintaining ships and their equipment from 1940 to 1966.

C

C & R: Abbreviation for Construction and Repair, referring to the department or equipment responsible for the ship's maintenance and damage control. The C&R air compressor was a low-pressure system used for various onboard tasks.

C.O.: Abbreviation for Commanding Officer, the officer in ultimate command of the submarine.

C.P.O.: Abbreviation for Chief Petty Officer, the senior-most group of enlisted personnel who act as technical experts and leaders.

ComPaseafron: Abbreviation for Commander, Panama Sea Frontier, the U.S. Navy command responsible for the defense of the sea approaches to the Panama Canal during World War II.

CSD: Abbreviation for Commander, Submarine Division, the officer in command of a group of submarines (e.g., CSD-31 for Submarine Division 31).

D

Depth Charges MK 17: A specific model of anti-submarine weapon, essentially a large canister of explosives designed to detonate at a pre-set depth to damage or destroy a submerged submarine.

E

Engine clutches: Mechanical devices that connect the submarine's diesel engines to the propeller shafts (for surface running) or to the electric motors/generators (for charging batteries). They allow for disengaging the engines during submerged operations.

F

Fuel oil tank: A tank within the submarine's hull used to store diesel fuel for the main engines.

G

Gyro compass: A non-magnetic compass that uses a fast-spinning gyroscope to find true north, providing a stable and accurate heading for navigation and torpedo targeting, regardless of the vessel's motion.

I

Inboard exhaust valve: A large valve located inside the pressure hull that seals the diesel engine exhaust line, preventing seawater from flooding the engine when the submarine is submerged.

Inner cones: Components of a cone-type engine clutch, which engage or disengage through friction to transmit power from the engine.

J

JK: An early type of passive sonar (hydrophone) used by U.S. submarines to listen for the sounds of propellers and machinery from other ships. The JK sound head was the underwater microphone component of this system.

M

Main Ballast Tank (M.B.T.): Large tanks located between the inner pressure hull and the outer hull of a submarine. Flooding them with water causes the submarine to submerge, and blowing the water out with compressed air causes it to surface.

Motor room escape trunk skirt: A flexible, rubberized canvas skirt at the bottom of the escape trunk. It is extended downwards to create a seal against the deck, allowing the trunk to be flooded and pressurized for crew escape without flooding the entire compartment.

O

O.O.D.: Abbreviation for Officer of the Deck, the officer on watch who is responsible for the safe navigation and operation of the submarine at any given time.

One hour dives: A routine dive, typically lasting an hour, conducted for training, trimming the boat, or remaining concealed during daylight hours in non-hostile waters.

P

PBY: Designation for the Consolidated PBY Catalina, a widely used American flying boat and amphibious aircraft. It served in anti-submarine patrol, reconnaissance, and search-and-rescue roles during World War II.

Q

QC: An early type of active sonar (echo-ranging) equipment used by U.S. surface ships and submarines. It transmitted a "ping" of sound and listened for the echo to determine the range and bearing of a submerged target.

Quick dives: A rapid submergence maneuver, often performed in under a minute, to evade detection by aircraft or surface ships.

R

Reserve lub oil tank: A storage tank holding a backup supply of lubricating oil for the submarine's engines and machinery.

S

Shifting collar: A mechanical component of a clutch assembly that is moved by a lever to engage or disengage the clutch plates or cones.

U

U.S. Army medium bomber: An aircraft such as a B-25 Mitchell or B-26 Marauder, operated by the U.S. Army Air Forces. These were sometimes used for maritime patrol and anti-submarine warfare.

U.S. Navy patrol bomber: A long-range aircraft, such as the PBY Catalina or PB4Y Liberator, used by the Navy for reconnaissance, anti-submarine patrols, and bombing missions over water.

V

Very star: A type of signal flare fired from a Very pistol. These flares, available in different colors, were used for communication and identification between ships and aircraft, especially at night.

Most Important Passages

Discovery of CRS Kickplate Light Reflection Issue

> *NOTE: It was found that CRS kickplates on conning tower ladder reflected light from control room. These were removed. A blanket was secured across inboard side of wardroom to permit reading this light on. (p. 6)*

Significance: This passage demonstrates tactical adaptation and problem-solving under operational conditions. The crew identified a security vulnerability where light from the control room was being reflected by metal kickplates, potentially compromising the submarine's position at night. The immediate corrective action shows attention to operational security details that could mean the difference between detection and survival.

Strategic Decision Against Calling Anti-Submarine Forces

> *The calling in of anti-submarine forces, planes and destroyers, was in the opinion of the Division Commander a sound decision. Holding on to the contact stubbornly would have been perhaps a more conspicuous act but the possibilities of destroying the enemy were greater by using those forces better equipped to do it. (p. 27)*

Significance: This passage reveals a critical command philosophy debate about submarine tactics. The Division Commander endorsed the decision to call in surface and air assets rather than pursue the enemy independently, reflecting the evolving doctrine of coordinated anti-submarine warfare and recognition of the limitations and strengths of different platforms.

Caribbean Sea Frontier Force Assignment

> *During the period covered by this report USS S-17 was operating as a unit of the Caribbean Sea Frontier Force. (p. 27)*

Significance: This establishes the strategic context of the patrol, showing that USS S-17 was part of the defensive network protecting vital Caribbean shipping lanes and the Panama Canal approaches. This was a critical theater for protecting oil shipments from Venezuela and maintaining supply lines.

Port Engine Flooding Casualty

> *The casualty whereby the port engine was flooded is one that could not readily be foreseen and was well and expeditiously handled. (p. 32)*

Significance: This passage addresses a serious mechanical failure that could have been catastrophic. The flooding of an engine compartment on a submarine represents a life-threatening emergency, and the commander's assessment that it was handled well indicates effective damage control training and crew performance under pressure.

Port Engine Clutch Failure and Repair

> *The port engine clutch was put out of commission because a brass wearing liner in the clutch shifting collar broke loose. It is secured to the shifting collar by means of studs. This liner then worked down into the clutch operating mechanism preventing the clutch from disengaging. Two clutches are being overhauled and steps are being taken to prevent a re-occurrence of this casualty. (p. 32)*

Significance: This detailed technical description documents a critical mechanical failure that disabled half the submarine's propulsion. The specific engineering details and corrective actions taken demonstrate the importance of mechanical reliability in submarine operations and the crew's ability to diagnose and address complex machinery problems.

Starboard Clutch Failure with Metal Debris

> *The starboard clutch became inoperative because one of the inner cones cracked and pieces of metal dropped into the operating mechanism. The damaged cone will be renewed. (p. 32)*

Significance: Coming after the port engine clutch failure, this second clutch failure represents a potentially catastrophic situation where the submarine lost propulsion capability on both engines. This highlights the mechanical challenges faced by older S-class submarines and the constant maintenance burden on crews.

Crew Morale Assessment After Fifth Patrol

> *The morale of the officers and crew were excellent upon return to port. (p. 32)*

Significance: Despite multiple mechanical failures and an uneventful patrol with no enemy contacts, the crew maintained excellent morale. This speaks to leadership quality and crew cohesion, which were essential for sustained submarine operations during extended patrols in challenging conditions.

Mine Field Navigation and Combat Readiness

> *Sortie through mine field was uneventful and course was set for the area (333°T). A skeleton gun's crew was stationed and kept on the instant alert during hours of darkness. Gun was cast lose and loaded and twelve rounds of ammunition were secured on deck. Gun's crew (pointer, trainer, gun captain, and loader, plus battery officer) were equipped*

with life jackets, and rubber boat was stowed on deck for immediate inflation in the event that ship was forced to dive with gun's crew on deck. (p. 37)

Significance: This passage illustrates the complex tactical considerations of submarine operations, including navigation through friendly minefields, maintaining surface gun readiness, and detailed safety procedures for deck crews. The preparation for emergency scenarios shows the constant balance between offensive capability and crew safety.

Depth Charge Attack Survival and Crew Response

After the bombs had struck the water a quiet interval of about four seconds (or less) was followed by three shocks within a quarter of a second of one another. The stern lifted several feet out of the water, the rising sensation being apparent on the bridge. The bow dipped sufficiently to bring the deck forward. The column of water to starboard did not quite come aboard and was not over fifty feet high. The port depth charges were seen to explode under the ship by one of the lookouts who actually observed a column of water to rise around the motor room and to fall back on deck. The book battery was approximately 20 yards, straddling the ship between the third and fourth bombs. (p. 58)

Significance: This vivid firsthand account of a depth charge attack provides crucial tactical intelligence about attack patterns and weapon effects. The detailed observations of timing, water column heights, and ship motion offer valuable data for understanding depth charge effectiveness and submarine survivability, while demonstrating the crew's ability to maintain observational discipline under attack.

Crew Habitability Improvements and Welfare Measures

Galley range was secured at lease one hour and a half before morning dive and not used during dive. Meal schedule found most satisfactory was breakfast for 0-4 and 4-8 watches at 0630. Cold lunch at 1200. Full meal was served after surfacing and cooking the food. It seems worth while to allow all hands to get about one hour fresh air in control room before serving this meal. A fine appetite results. (No sandwiches are allowed after 1730 to further insure good meal supplies at this daily full meal). Battery charge is secured two hours before morning dive to afford time for ventilating to cool. A blower is placed on resistors during all charges, and until dive, to assure most effective heat dissipation. Battery blowers are invariably run full speed whenever boat is on surface in order to keep battery as cool as possible. (p. 43)

Significance: This detailed description of daily routines reveals the human side of submarine operations and the careful attention to crew welfare. The meal scheduling, ventilation procedures, and temperature management demonstrate how commanders balanced operational requirements with crew health and morale, recognizing that well-fed and comfortable crews performed better during long patrols.

War Patrol Reports

START OF REEL

JOB NO. G-108 / AR-45-80

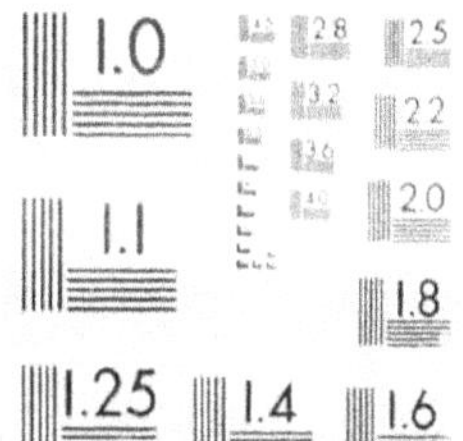

OPERATOR M. Monroe

DATE 3/14/80

THIS MICROFILM IS THE PROPERTY OF THE UNITED STATES GOVERNMENT

MICROFILMED BY
NPPSO–NAVAL DISTRICT WASHINGTON
MICROFILM SECTION

REEL TARGET - START AND END
NDW-NPPSO-5210/1 (6-78)

S-17 (SS-122)

WORLD WAR II FILE

ALL MATERIAL ON THIS REEL IS DECLASSIFIED

FOR DECK LOG THROUGH 4 OCTOBER 1944 CONSULT NATIONAL ARCHIVES WHICH HAS CUSTODY.

S-17

(SS-122: dp. 876 (surf.), 1,092 (subm.); l. 231'; b. 21'10"; dr. 13'1"; s. 15 k. (surf.), 11 k. (subm.); cpl. 38; a. 4 21" tt., 1 4"; cl. *S-3*)

S-17 (SS-122) was laid down on 19 March 1918 by the Lake Torpedo Boat Co., Bridgeport, Conn.; launched on 22 May 1920; sponsored by Mrs. Raymond G. Thomas; and commissioned on 1 March 1921, Lt. Comdr. Charles S. Alden in command.

Departing from New London, Conn., on 31 May 1921, *S-17* sailed via the Panama Canal, California, Hawaii, and Guam to the Philippines, arriving at Cavite, Luzon, on 1 December. In 1922, she sailed from Manila Bay on 11 October, visited Hong Kong from the 14th to the 28th, and returned to Cavite on 1 November. Sailing from Manila on 15 May 1923, *S-17* visited Shanghai, Chefoo, and Chinwangtao, before returning via Woosung and Amoy to Cavite on 11 September. In the summer of 1924, she visited Shanghai, Tsingtao, Chefoo, and Chinwangtao, before returning via Chefoo and Amoy to Olongapo, Luzon, on 23 September. Departing Cavite on 29 October, she arrived at Mare Island, Calif., on 31 December.

Remaining at Mare Island in 1925 and 1926, she operated along the California coast in 1927, mainly at Mare Island, San Diego, and San Pedro. From February 1928 into December 1934, *S-17* served in the Panama Canal area. Departing from Coco Solo on 10 December 1934, *S-17* was decommissioned on 29 March 1935 at Philadelphia.

S-17 was recommissioned on 16 December 1940. After voyages to Bermuda, *S-17* operated in the Panama Canal area from December 1941 into February 1942; at St. Thomas in March; in the Panama Canal area from April into August; and out of New London from September that year into July 1944. Her cruises from New London often included operations at Casco Bay, Maine. Decommissioned on 4 October 1944, *S-17* was struck from the Navy list on 13 November of that year and was intentionally sunk on 5 April 1945.

Dictionary of

American Naval Fighting Ships

VOLUME VI

Historical Sketches—Letters R through S

Appendices—Submarine Chasers (SC)
Eagle-Class Patrol Craft (PE)

WITH A FOREWORD BY
ADMIRAL JAMES L. HOLLOWAY III, United States Navy,
THE CHIEF OF NAVAL OPERATIONS

AND AN INTRODUCTION BY
VICE ADMIRAL EDWIN B. HOOPER, United States Navy, Retired,
THE DIRECTOR OF NAVAL HISTORY

NAVAL HISTORY DIVISION
DEPARTMENT OF THE NAVY
WASHINGTON: 1976

SUBMARINE DIVISION ~~SEVENTY-TWO~~ THIRTY-TWO

A12-1 (08) U.S.S. S-11 , Flagship
c/o Postmaster, New York, New York

CONFIDENTIAL

14 January 1942.

From: Commander Submarine Division Thirty-Two.
To: Chief of Naval Operations.
Commander-in-Chief, United States Fleet.
Commander Submarines, Atlantic Fleet.

SUBJECT: War Diary of USS S-17 covering Patrol in Pacific Area off Costa Rica from 10 December 1941 to 30 December 1941.

1. In accordance with Operation Order No. 39-41, issued by Commander Panama Naval Coastal Frontier Force, the S-17 left Coco Solo on 10 December, three days after the attack on Pearl Harbor and proceed to patrol station.

2. The following Commanding Officer's war diary is forwarded:

<u>Wednesday, 10 December 1941.</u>

1415 Underway from Coco Solo, proceeding on assigned patrol.
1455 Received Panama Canal pilot and commenced transit of Panama Canal.
2210 Dropped Panama Canal pilot and received mine field pilot.
2315 Dropped pilot and set course 180° true, standard speed both engines.

<u>Thursday, 11 December 1941.</u>

0001 Passed Bona Island light abeam to starboard.
0640 Passed Cape Mala light abeam to starboard.
0745 Changed course to left to investigate derelict. Turned out to be small dug-out, partially flooded.
0755 Set course 200° true.
0910 Made trim dive; surfaced 1055.
1345 Sighted steamer distance about 7 miles; made quick dive and commenced approach. Steamer turned out to be a fishing boat of about 30 tons. 1650 fishing boat passed over horizon.
1652 Surfaced and set course 200° true.
1900 Stopped starboard engine and commenced battery charge; continued at 2/3 speed on port engine.

SUBMARINE DIVISION ~~SEVENTY-TWO~~ THIRTY-TWO

A12-1 (08) U. S. S. S-11 , Flagship
c/o Postmaster, New York, New York

CONFIDENTIAL

14 January 1942.

SUBJECT: War Diary of USS S-17 coveri g Patrol in Pacific Area off Costa Rica from 1C ecember 1941 to 30 December 1941.

- -

Friday, 12 December 1941.

0400 Secured battery charge, and went ahead on both engines, 2/3 speed.
1358 Sighted plane believed to be Army P-40; made quick dive.
1935 Surfaced (dusk).
1946 Went ahead standard on both engines.
2015 Changed course to 270° true.

NOTE: It was found that CRS kickplates on conning tower ladder reflected light from control room. These were removed. A blanket was secured across inboard side of wardroom to permit keeping this light on.

Saturday, 13 December 1941.

0750 Sighted ship one point on starboard bow, distance approximately 6 miles; made quick dive.
0910 Surfaced, went ahead 1/3 on both engines.
0925 Went ahead 2/3 on both engines.
0930 Went ahead standard speed on both engines.

Sunday, 14 December 1941.

0725 Changed course to 000° true.
0800 Changed course to 315° true.
1140 Changed course to 270° true.
2000 Stopped port engine.
No sights. No contacts. Sea moderate.

Monday, 15 December 1941.

1100 Made trim dive; surfaced at 1158.
1205 Went ahead 2/3 speed on both engines and set course 270°.
2300 Set course 285° true.

Tuesday, 16 December 1941.

0800 Set course 270° true.
1815 Arrived on station; changed course to 090° true; slowed to 1/3 speed on both engines and put on 250 ampere parallel float.

SUBMARINE DIVISION ~~SEVENTY-TWO~~ THIRTY-TWO

A12-1 (08) U. S. S. S-11 , Flagship

c/o Postmaster, New York, New York

CONFIDENTIAL

14 January 1942.

SUBJECT: War Diary USS S-17 covering Patrol in Pacific Area off Costa Rica from 10 December 1941 to 30 December 1941.

- -

Wednesday, 17 December 1941.

0100 Secured float; changed course to 270° true. Stopped port engine and went ahead 2/3 on starboard engine.
1019 Made trim dive. 1100 Surfaced and went ahead 1/3 on both engines. 1130 went ahead 2/3 on both engines.
1915 Changed course to 215° true.
1929 Stopped starboard engine, commenced battery charge, went ahead 2/3 on port engine.
2000 Changed course to 270° true.
2300 Secured battery charge.

Thursday, 18 December 1941.

0100 Changed course to 090° true.
0730 Changed course to 270° true.
0810 Had steering casualty; shifted to hand steering.
0838 Returned steering to electrical control in conning tower.
2230 Changed course to 090° true.

Friday, 19 December 1941.

0830 Changed course to 270° true.
1008 Made quick dive for trim; surfaced at 1035.
1040 Went ahead 1/3 on both engines.
1045 Went ahead 2/3 on both engines.
1105 Stopped starboard engine, commenced battery charge.
2200 Changed course to 090° true.

Saturday, 20 December 1941.

0005 Completed battery charge, stopped starboard engine.
0900 Changed course to 270° true.
1250 Sighted plane believed to be VS Navy patrol bomber; made quick dive; surfaced 1340; went ahead 1/3 speed on both engines.
1419 Went ahead 2/3 speed on both engines.
1600 Stopped starboard engine; changed course to 090° true.

3.

3

SUBMARINE DIVISION ~~SEVENTY-TWO~~ THIRTY-TWO

A12-1 (08) U. S. S. S-11 , Flagship
c/o Postmaster, New York, New York

CONFIDENTIAL

14 January 1942.

SUBJECT: War Diary USS S-17 covering Patrol in Pacific Area off Costa Rica from 10 December 1941 to 30 December 1941.

- -

Sunday, 21 December 1941.

0005 Changed course to 270° true.
1358 Changed course to 090° true.
1900 Commenced battery charge (600 ampere parallel float) on both engines.
2200 Secured 600 ampere float and stopped starboard engine. Went ahead 2/3 speed on port engine.

Monday, 22 December 1941.

0300 Changed course to 270° true.
0956 Made trim dive; surfaced at 1033 and went ahead 1/3 speed on both engines.
1104 Stopped port engine and went ahead 2/3 on starboard engine.
1500 Changed course to 090° true.
1930 Changed speed to 1/3 speed on both engines and commenced a 650 ampere parallel float.
2030 Changed course to 100° true.

Tuesday, 23 December 1941.

0030 Changed course to 090° true.
0230 Changed course to 270° true.
0700 Stopped starboard engine.
1130 Changed course to 090° true, went ahead 2/3 on both engines.
1146 Changed course to 270° true.
1558 Changed course to 090° true.
1930 Changed speed to 1/3 on both engines and commenced 600 ampere parallel float.

Wednesday, 24 December 1941.

0200 Secured float, stopped port engine and went ahead 2/3 on starboard engine; changed course to 270° true.
1310 Made trim dive; surfaced at 1348 and went ahead 2/3 speed on port engine; changed course to 090° true.

SUBMARINE DIVISION ~~SEVENTY-TWO~~ THIRTY-TWO

A12-1 (08) U. S. S. S-11 , Flagship
c/o Postmaster, New York, New York

CONFIDENTIAL

14 January 1942.

SUBJECT: War Diary USS S-17 covering Patrol in Pacific Area off Costa Rica from 10 December 1941 to 30 December 1941.

- -

1900 Slowed to 1/3 speed on port engine and went ahead 1/3 on starboard engine carrying 600 ampere parallel float.
2300 Secured float; stopped starboard engine.
2310 Changed course to 270° true.

Thursday, 25 December 1941.

1100 Sighted plane believed to be Army patrol plane and made quick dive.
1203 Came up to periscope depth and scanned horizon.
1302 Surfaced, went ahead on motors.
1310 Went ahead 2/3 speed on both engines.
1325 Took a suction through the boat. Had man standing by to close torpedo room hatch on word from bridge; secured at 1335.
1800 Changed course to 090° true.

Friday, 26 December 1941.

0300 Changed course to 270° true.
1500 Changed c ourse to 090° true.
2030 Went ahead 2/3 speed on both engines and put on 800 ampere parallel float.
2305 Changed course to 100° true.

Saturday, 27 December 1941.

0000 Went ahead standard speed on both engines. Secured charge.
0700 Changed course to 090° true.
1445 Slowed to 2/3 speed on both engines.
1605 Went ahead standard speed on both engines.

Sunday, 28 December 1941.

0500 Changed speed to 2/3 on both engines.
0800 Sighted Army flying fortress and fired smoke bomb. Plane flew fairly close aboard and then turned away.
1143 Sighted Army bomber; fired smoke bomb.

SUBMARINE DIVISION ~~SEVENTY-TWO~~ THIRTY-TWO

A12-1 (08) U. S. S. S-11 , Flagship
c/o Postmaster, New York, New York

CONFIDENTIAL

14 January 1942.

SUBJECT: War Diary of USS S-17 covering Patrol in Pacific Area off Costa Rica from 10 December 1941 to 30 December 1941.

- -

1705 Made trim dive; surfaced at 1737, and went ahead 2/3 on both engines.
1815 Secured port engine for dive.

Monday, 29 December 1941.

0500 Went ahead 2/3 on port engine and stopped starboard engine.
1438 Sighted steamer bearing 056° true, distance about eight miles, changed course to 270° true.
1510 Commenced circling to allow steamer to pass over horizon.
1558 Steadied on course 270° true.
1610 Changed course to 090° true.
2030 Changed course to 070° true.

Tuesday, 30 December 1941.

0030 Changed course to 080° true.
0550 Sighted land broad on port bow.
0730 Changed course to 105° true.
1032 Sighted and identified USS BONITA; fired smoke bomb.
1055 Sighted and identified USS BARRACUDA bearing 350° true, distance six miles.
1330 Sighted Navy PBY plane on port quarter; fired smoke bomb (Smoke bomb failed to fire).
1558 Changed course to 090° true.
1726 Sighted and identified S-11.
1840 2/3 speed on both engines.
1841 Ahead standard speed on both engines.
2100 Chnaged course to 020° true.

Wednesday, 31 December 1941.

0030 Slowed to 2/3 speed on both engines.
0408 Changed course to North.
0542 Sighted Cape Mala lighthouse broad on port bow, distance about 10 miles.
0700 Sighted escort vessel.
0715 Gained escort vessel and arrived at rendevous of S-11, 6

SUBMARINE DIVISION THIRTY-TWO ~~SEVENTY-TWO~~

A12-1 (08) U. S. S. S-11 , Flagship

c/o Postmaster, New York, New York

CONFIDENTIAL

14 January 1942.

SUBJECT: War Diary of USS S-17 covering patrol in Pacific Area off Costa Rica from 10 December 1941 to 30 December 1941.

- -

BARRACUDA and BONITA; formed column and proceeded at eight knots on course 028° true.

F. B. LONGSTAFF.

Copy to:

Comsubron 3.

7.

7

A12-1
Serial 01,
CONFIDENTIAL

U. S. S. S-17,
c/o Postmaster,
New York, New York,
4 February 1942.

From: Commanding Officer.
To: Commander Submarine Division Thirty-Two.

SUBJECT: War Diary of USS S-17 for Patrol Period 15 January - 2 February 1942.

Enclosure: (a) Logistic Data for Patrol.

1. A war patrol was conducted by this submarine during the period noted pursuant to Commander Submarine, Offshore Patrol, Pacific, secret mailgram 130900 of January 13, 1942.

2. Departed Submarine Base, Coco Solo, at 1510, on 15 January, transited Panama Canal and moored to pier 18, Balboa. Joined formation with S-42, S-43, S-45 and S-46 off Canal entrance buoys and proceeded toward point "A" under escort. Made trim dive enroute. At 1349 on 17 January the only material casualty worthy of note occurred when a fitting on fuel line to starboard engine carried away and forced a shut down. At this time it was decided to renew one exhaust valve cage on the port engine. All engines were secured for two hours; repairs effected and course and speed regained. By this time the accompanying submarines had passed out of sight so remainder of patrol was made independently. Patrol station was gained and departure made pursuant to operation order. First contact on return was made with S-46 at approximately 0200, Friday, 30 January. Made rendezvous at designated point at 0700 on 1 February and returned to base in company with other submarines. Arrived Coco Solo at 0625 on 2 February.

3. The initial point of the patrol station was latitude 9° N., longitude 93° W. The patrol was normally a surface one, steaming to westward during daylight and retiring during darkness.

4. No events of note occurred.

5. No action or contact with enemy forces occurred.

6. Torpedo tubes were not flooded during the patrol. All torpedoes were backed out of tubes, inspected, and topped off each five days. Maximum loss of air noted was 250 lbs.

7. In general the weather was excellent, visibility high. For three days the sea was sufficiently rough to make control at periscope depth difficult. No rain was encountered.

40024 - Filmed

A12-1
Serial 01.

U.S.S. S-17

4 February 1942.

CONFIDENTIAL

SUBJECT: War Diary of USS S-17 for Patrol Period 15 January - 2 February 1942.

- -

8. Habitability was good.

9. The health of the crew was excellent with two exceptions; one man was transferred at Balboa, diagnosis catarrhal fever. The other man suffered a sinus irritation four days out and was confined to his bunk for the remainder of the patrol. He was sent back to duty by the doctor immediately upon return to the Submarine Base. The morale was excellent. Food was ample, with an estimated 14 days supply on hand at end of patrol. Boredom is the most adverse factor to be overcome on a patrol like this. Crew is now sufficiently expert so that dives are made in 50 seconds from diving alarm. This interval, plus the 3 or 4 seconds required between sighting a plane and sounding the diving alarm, makes this type boat capable of disappearing within one minute of sighting an enemy plane or vessel. Greater speed is obtainable, but the limiting factor is clearing the bridge of men.

10. It was noted that water running into the free flooding superstructure and cascading out through the small holes caused the formation of a very white band of frothy water which served to outline the hull. It is this whiteness on the surface of the ocean which usually calls an aviators attention to the presence of a submarine. This characteristic may be overcome by cutting away large enough sections of the solid side superstructure plating so that only a skeleton remains. Water running in and out will then have no tendency to froth.

B J Harral

B. J. HARRAL.

2

U.S.S. S-17

Enclosure (A) to USS S-17 ltr. A12-1 (01) of 4 February 1942.

LOGISTIC DATA

War Patrol - 15 January - 2 February 1942.

	January.								
Date:	15	16	17	18	19	20	21	22	23
Fuel used (gals)	240	420	1380	1080	1040	980	710	680	460
Fuel on hand 2400	32627	32207	30827	29747	28707	27727	27017	26337	25877
Lub used	240	10	120	65	110	120	15	140	15
Lub on hand 2400	4342	4332	4212	4147	4037	3917	3902	3762	3747
Fresh water used	50	225	200	195	215	175	210	[illegible]	275
Water distilled	0	0	0	0	0	0	0	0	0
Water on hand 2400	4150	3925	3725	3530	3315	3140	2930	2605	2330
Hours C&R A.C. run	0	0	0	0	2	2	4	3	5
Battery water used	0	0	0	0	0	0	0	0	0
Battery water on hand 2400	850	850	850	850	850	850	850	850	850
Provisions on hand *(fresh)	5	4	3	2	1	0	0	0	0
Provisions on hand dry (days)	35	34	33	32	31	30	29	28	27

*Governing factor in this item was fresh vegetables, not fresh meat.

3

U.S.S. S-17

Enclosure (A) to S-17 ltr. A12-1 (01) of 4 February 1942.

CONFIDENTIAL

LOGISTIC DATA

War Patrol - 15 January - 2 February 1942.

Date:	January. 24	25	26	27	28	29	30	41	Feb. 1
Fuel used (gals)	680	640	550	530	860	1150	1220	1170	650
Fuel on hand 2400	25197	24557	24007	23477	22617	21467	17947	16777	16127
Lub used	160	90	.15	115	75	130	130	120	20
Lub on hand 2400	3587	3497	3482	3367	3292	3162	3032	2912	2892
Fresh water used	225	225	150	275	125	78	225	210	200
Water distilled	0	0	0	0	0	0	0	0	0
Water on hand 2400	2005	1780	1630	1355	1105	1027	802	592	392
Hours C&R A.C. run	6	6	6	2	2	2	0	0	0
Battery water used	0	0	0	0	0	0	0	0	450
Battery water on hand 2400	850	850	850	850	850	850	850	850	400
Provisions on hand * (fresh)	0	0	0	0	0	0	0	0	0
Provisions on hand dry (days)	26	25	24	23	22	21	20	19	18

*Governing factor in this item was fresh vegetables, not fresh meat.

REMARKS

Watered batteries while transiting the Canal.

SUBMARINE DIVISION ~~SEVENTY-TWO~~ THIRTY-TWO

A12-1 (013) U. S. S. S-11 , Flagship

c/o Postmaster, New York, New York

CONFIDENTIAL

1st Endorsement to
S-17 ltr. A12-1
(01) of 2/4/42

9 February 1942.

From: Commander Submarine Division Thirty-Two.
To : Commander-in-Chief, United States Fleet.
Commander-in-Chief, Atlantic Fleet.
Commander Submarines, Atlantic Fleet.

SUBJECT: War Diary of USS S-17 for Patrol Period 15 January - 2 February 1942.

1. Forwarded.

J. B. LONGSTAFF.

Copy to:

Comsubron 3
Comsubdiv 31.

5

C-O-P-Y

U. S. S. S-17 (SS-122)
SUBMARINE DIVISION 43

SS122/A16

Serial 06-42

C/o Postmaster,
New York City,
March 6, 1942.

From: The Commanding Officer, U.S.S. S-17
To : The Commander Submarines, Atlantic Fleet.
Via : The Commander Submarine Division THIRTY-TWO.

Subject: War Diary, 28 February - 6th March 1942.

1. First day out exercise was conducted with a plane (31-P-4) of VP31 to test effectiveness of plane radar and voice communication with plane, surface and submerged. Results indicate that effective range was about 6 to 8 miles when submarine ran with about three feet of free board. However, when running with all main ballast tanks full, riding safety and bow buoyancy vents, and the conning tower only showing, effective range was reduced to less than one mile. This extreme flooded down condition was therefore adopted, very fortunately as it later turned out, for all surface cruising. Voice communications with plane on 7965 Kcs. was successful both surface and submerged.

Later the same day, an American Marine plane dropped a 100 lb. bomb aimed at our periscope. Noise was not sufficient to be picked up by JK. Upon surfacing, a Marine plane failed to understand recognition signal and dropped a 100 lb. bomb within 50 yards of the boat. Two officers on the bridge were uninjured, and no fragments came aboard. Noise of explosion came through the hull very distinctly.

Second day in Anegada Passage.

Picked up a U.S. destroyer and plane escort on JK range 8,000 yds. observed through periscope, then dove to 175 feet, stopped all machinery except gyro and JK and departed from area on one screw, dead slow. Apparently was unheard by DD. No pinging observed.

Third day.

At 0756, while at 80 feet, the JK man reported distinct but weak signals from a ship which he assumed to be a submarine. Changed course from 040° to 020° to 330°, and true bearing remained essentially the same. Came up to periscope depth, saw nothing on the horizon, went back to 80 feet; ran quiet. Occasional noises which might have been pings were heard. For one hour ship was maneuvered in an effort to lose contact, but this was not successful, as the enemy seemed desirous of maintaining contact.

WHY?

-1-

RECORDED [initials]

C-O-P-Y

U. S. S. S-17
SUBMARINE DIVISION 43

March 6, 1942

SS122/A16

Serial 06-42

C-O-N-F-I-D-E-N-T-I-A-L

Subject: War Diary, 28 February - 6th March 1942.

- -

At the end of this time it was decided to reverse course, put enemy ahead, and attempt to ram. This effort was persisted in for 35 minutes without success. It was now decided to leave the area, so short bursts of high speed on several headings were resorted to, and all contact was lost by the end of 20 minutes.

FIFTH DAY

On this morning ship was cruising with decks submerged as usual, Port engine secured, starboard ahead 2/3. Base course 148° (T) zig-zagging radically. At 0532, just at the beginning of morning twilight a lookout reported "Ship or submarine on port bow". The O.O.D. immediately picked up the object with his glasses and recognized at an estimated range of 3500 or 4000 yards, a submarine flooded down, the white water on deck clearly visible. Details were difficult to distinguish, but size was definitely believed to be about 1000 tons, very low bridge rail, and low periscope shears. Silhouette was not very large.

Bridge was immediately cleared, engine speeded up to standard and when Commanding Officer arrived on the bridge an instant later, the O.O.D. had already decided to turn away and prepare to dive. Range was too great for torpedo run. Commanding Officer did not see the enemy but immediately sounded the diving alarm. At 0534 periscope depth was passed. The enemy was not picked up by periscope, it being still very dark. Dove to sixty feet, slowed, and at 0535 steadied on course 300° (T).

JK immediately reported sound of screws on 170° relative. All machinery was stopped except starboard screw, depth 60 feet. Following sound data taken:

Ping first heard with our JK oscillator "off". Consisted of single power note with reverberations.

Oscillator was switched to "on" and picked up a CW note whose frequency varied within the audio range as though driven with an automatic frequency sweep. Audible frequency changed from an 800 cycle pitch to 400 cycle pitch during keying interval which persisted for about one/fifth second. Hetrodyne frequency on during this time was set at midpoint (approx. 85 kcs). No propellors (?) distinguished thistime. His propellor noises were very distinct and loud. Estimated speed 250 to 300 4.p.m.

-2-

C-O-P-Y

U.S.S. S-17
SUBMARINE DIVISION 43

March 6, 1942

SS122/A6
Serial 06-42

C-O-N-F-I-D-E-N-T-I-A-L

Subject: War Diary, 28 February - 6th March 1942.

- -

Next his propeller noise suddenly ceased. Numerous pings were recorded, occasionally accompanied by power note. During this time our screws were toward him, and motors were now speeded up to normal series. He continued pinging for about a minute longer. Total pings about 20.

Next a buzz was heard all around the dial and it shortly seemed to fade out forward. This may be explained as the result of either; an electrical counter-sound interference to confuse our sound bearings, or a rather slow speed torpedo which passed fairly close aboard.

Now (0542) changed course to 270° to give best de-gaussed protection in the event he fired a torpedo with magnetic exploder. Continued speed for about five minutes, then changed course to 180° (T), and ran on one motor parallel all machinery dead. Nothing further was heard.

Came to periscope depth (0552), could see nothing. Course was changed back to 270°, and speed of 1.8 knots held for one hour, during which time contact reported was encoded. Surfaced at 0745, all ahead standard speed, radioed in report. Cleared the area at standard speed for one hour so as not to hamper aircraft anti-submarine work.

It was considered that this submarine was returning to Europe and would make a submerged land-fall, on Sombrero Light Tower, which is visible for 18 miles at periscope depth.

This second submarine contact convinces me that enemy submarines are using Anegada Passage for entrance and exit into the Caribbean area. This passage is wide and deep and Sombero presents a magnificent land-fall, night or day. It is strongly recommended that this light be extinguished and this tower be demolished.

It is somewhat difficult to explain how this vessel was able to make first contact with a German submarine which was undoubtedly equipped with radar and sufface listening. However, practice with aircraft radar indicated that submarine was vastly harder to pick up in this low freeboard condition as compared with a condition of three feet freeboard.

This experience very sharply accents the advisibility of reducing the unnecessarily large silhouette presented by present U.S. Submarine construction.

C-O-P-Y

U. S. S. S-17
SUBMARINE DIVISION 43

March 6, 1942

SS122/A16
Serial 06-42

February - 6 March.

2. Excellent.

3. None.

4. It has been noted in (1) that Sombrero Light is a great help to enemy submarines entering the Caribbean, and should be extinguished and the tower demolished.

5. See (1).

6. Sighted two Marine amphibian planes from Bourne Field. In both instances their presence was indicated by JK operator who reported a "high speed noise".

7. None made.

8. See remarks in (1).

9. None not already recognized as inherent in this type of submarine.

10. Radio reception excellent. In one case an urgent message for San Juan had to be relayed via Washington. Sound conditions were superior at greater depths. Habitability was satisfactory during the fivesuccessive thirteen hour dives. Endurance of boat for such submerged patrol is believed to be about fourteen to seventeen days.

Copies to:
✓Com North Atlantic
Anti-Sub Patrol (1)
Naval Exp. Lab. Bellevue. (1)
Comsubdiv 32 Org. & 6.

B. J. HARRAL.

031455 March CONFIDENTIAL ROUTINE CCSF to OPNAV

Small caliber shelling Mona Island 0830 Q last night x Believe U-Boat going north.

032240 March CONFIDENTIAL URGENT S-17 to TG 26.3

Maintained sound contact with submarine course southerly from 7 to 900 posit 30 miles southeast Anegada Island x Request instructions.

040122 CONFIDENTIAL URGENT CTG 26.3 to SOMERS

S-17 patrolling between Anegada Island and Sombero Island.

051945 CONFIDENTIAL ROUTINE CTG 26.3 to CINCLANT

Request authority use 4135 series for communications between task group commander x Submarines and surface craft this group x Distances involve up to 600 miles.

040115 March Confidential OPPRI From 26.3.5 To S-17 Info 26.3
Marine Planes Scouting Anegada Passage Tonight x Submerge on Approach

S-17 WAR DAIRY

Afternoon 2/28 Marine plane bombed S-17. Not picked up by JK. Upon surfacing, a Marine plane failed to understand recognition signal and dropped a 100 lb bomb within 50 yards of S-17.

3/1 Picked up a U.S. Destroyer and plane escort on JK range 8000 yds. Dove to 175', stopped all machinery, departed area. Apparently DD did not hear.

3/2 At 0756, at 80', JK operator reported weak but distinct signals from a ship which he assumed a submarine. Came up to periscope depth, saw nothing, went back to 80'. For 1 hr. tried to lose contact from what S-17 thought might have been pings. At end of this time, reversed course to ram. Tried 35 minutes without success. Left area. Contact lost at end of 20 minutes.

3/4 Cruising on surface on course 148° T. zig-zagging, at 0532 when picked up submarine 3500-4000 yds on port bow. O.O.D. turned away and prepared to dive. C.O. did not see SS, but immediately sounded diving alarm. At 0534 periscope depth was passed. Dove to 60', slowed, and at 0535 steadied on course 300° T. JK reported sound of screws on 170° relative.

0542 c.c. to 270° T. to protect from magnetic torpedo. Continued for about 5 minutes, then changed course to 180° T. Nothing further was heard.

At 0552 came to periscope depth, saw nothing, cc to 270°, speed 1.8 kts. held for 1 hour, during which time contact reported was encoded. Surfaced at 0745, all ahead standard, radioed in report. Cleared area at standard speed for one hour so as not to hamper aircraft anti-submarine work.

Radio reception excellent. In one case URGENT message for San Juan had to be relayed via Washington. Sound conditions were superior at greater depths.

20.

1. Failure of recognition signal merits special attention.
2. Detecting planes on JK interesting - should be investigated by ComSubs.
3. Encoding of contact report under these circumstances may have been a contributing cause for failure to get planes out and get the sub.

Suggest we wait to see what action ComSubs will take on these points.

13.

Note on page 1, persistent effort to lose contact with "enemy submarine".
Note Fifth Day operations were certainly lacking in aggressiveness.

Recommend we ask ComSubs to comment.

16.

It appears that this submarine did not take prompt or effective action to either:-
1. Attack enemy.
2. Report Contact.

Recommend that action by CinCLant be deferred pending action which it is assumed will be taken by ComSubDiv 32 and ComSubsLant.

Also note use of JK to detect approach of planes - (Para. 6, page 4.)

THIRTY-TWO
SUBMARINE DIVISION ~~SEVENTY-TWO~~

A12-1 (030) U. S. S. S-11 , Flagship
[illegible] Postmaster, New York, New York

1st Endorsement to
S-17 ltr. A16 (06)
of 3/6/42.

15 April 1942.

From: Commander Submarine Division Thirty-Two.
To: Commanding Officer, U.S.S. S-17.

SUBJECT: War Diary - 28 February-6 March 1942.

1. Returned for further information.

2. It is noted that on both occasions of assumed enemy contact you state that you maneuvered your ship to avoid contact. The reason for this departure from the agressive action normally expected is not given. By endorsement please explain any material or personnel conditions that influenced your decision not to attack immediately.

J. B. LONGSTAFF.

File No.

SS122/A16

Serial 06-42

U. S. S. S-17

SECOND ENDORSEMENT to
[illegible] A16 (06)

c/o Postmaster,
New York City.

CONFIDENTIAL

DECLASSIFIED - OPNAV INST 5500.30
BY [illegible] DATE 4 AUG 59

April 29, 1942.

From: The Commanding Officer.
To: The Commander Submarine Division [illegible]-TWO.

Subject: War Diary - 2[illegible] February - 6 March 1942.

1. The first contact by sound was made on bearing 160° rel. ship's head 040° (T). In the succeeding process of maneuvering to develope the sound bearing, and of searching with the periscope, nearly sixty minutes were consumed. It was at this time that a determined effort was made to ram. The fruitlessness of attempting to ram a submerged submarine with another submerged submarine soon became apparent. I therefore broke off the contact and left the area.

2. The second contact was made beyond torpedo range. The officer of the deck appreciated this and chose not to waste a torpedo. The enemy immediately dove and left me no alternative but to dive also. It was still too dark for a periscope attack so that was out of the question. My previous experience has convinced me that ramming submerged is not feasible. There was no apparent alternative except to send out a contact report as soon as possible so that Carib Sea Frontier anti-submarine forces would be enabled to take proper action.

3. In case "I", I was able to swiftly break off contact when I so desired as shown by report. The wording "for one hour ship was maneuvered in an effort to lose contact" is misleading.

4. In case "II", I fail to see how an attack could have been made that would have been justified under present conditions of limited torpedo supply.

Brooks Harral.

War Diary
DM

SUBMARINE DIVISION SEVENTY-TWO THIRTY-TWO

A12-1 (032) U. S. S. S-11 , Flagship
c/o Postmaster, New York, New York

3rd Endorsement to
S-17 ltr. A16 (06)

6 May 1942.

From: Commander Submarine Division Thirty-Two.
To: Commander Submarines, Atlantic Fleet.
Via: Commander Submarine Squadron Three.

SUBJECT: USS S-17 Patrol Report for the period 28 February - 6 March 1942.

1. Forwarded. This is a patrol report rather than a war diary and the paragraphs are numbered in accordance with Commander Submarines, Pacific Fleet, Confidential Letter No. 12-41

2. The basic report was returned by endorsement for further information and explanation. The wording of this report might give the impression that action was refused and escape was the primary thought.

3. The character of the Commanding Officer is such that aggressive action would be more natural than withdrawal and it was apparent that some circumstances not made clear in the report must have caused a deviation from this policy.

4. In the second endorsement the Commanding Officer gives his reasons for breaking off the contact.

5. There is some doubt that contact No.1 on the third day was an actual contact. Thirty-five minutes of various speeds toward an enemy submarine, persistently trying to keep contact, would have brought the two submarines quite close together. It required only twenty minutes of evasive tactics to lose the contact.

6. The second contact, that on the fifth morning, appears quite definitely to have been a submarine. Both ships submerged and from then on the only contact was by sound. The S-17 has no echo ranging device, the enemy presumably had. That one piece of equipment contributes greatly to the effectiveness of any submerged tactics. With the depth of the enemy as well as the range unknown, the expenditure of torpedoes was not justified.

1.

THIRTY-TWO
SUBMARINE DIVISION ~~SEVENTY-TWO~~

A12-1 (032) U. S. S. S-11 , Flagship
c/o Postmaster, New York, New York

CONFIDENTIAL

SUBJECT: S-17 Patrol Report for the period 28 February - 6 March 1942.

- -

The calling in of anti-submarine forces, planes and destroyers, was in the opinion of the Division Commander a sound decision. Holding on to the contact stubbornly would have been perhaps a more conspicious act but the possibilities of destroying the enemy were greater by using those forces better equipped to do it.

C. H. LOBSTAFF.

Copy to: S-17

- -

FOURTH ENDORSEMENT	SUBMARINE SQUADRON THREE	Coco Solo, C.Z.
FF4-3/A16-1	U. S. S. S-13 - Flagship	May 9, 1942

Serial 093

From: Commander Submarine Squadron Three.
To : Commander Submarines, Atlantic Fleet.

1. Forwarded.

2. During the period covered by this report USS S-17 was operating as a unit of the Caribbean Sea Frontier Force.

T. J. DOYLE.

1st copy

U.S.S. S-17 - REPORT OF FOURTH WAR PATROL

Period from 15 May 1942 to 4 June 1942.

Area: Inner Patrol Area, Panama Naval Sea Frontier.

Operation Order: Comsubsoffshorepatpac mailgram 071500 as modified by his mailgram 221817.

1. Narrative.

0708 - 15 May - Underway from Balboa, C.Z., in accordance with operation order, enroute to patrol area.
1218 - 19 May - On patrol station.
0800 - 2 June - Departed patrol area for Gulf of Dulce.

2. Weather overcast with south westerly winds and very frequent rain squalls. Seas and wind moderate on the whole.

3. Experienced a constant easterly set of from 0.5 to 1.0 knots.

4. - - - -

5. - - - -

6. Sighted aircraft as follows:

Date	Time	Number	Type
16 May	1423	1	U.S. Army medium bomber.
18 May	1030	2	U.S. Army bombers.
21 May	1305	1	U.S. Navy patrol bomber.
23 May	0943	2	U.S. Army bombers.
25 May	1151	1	Unidentified plane
26 May	1210	1	Unidentified plane
1 June	0952	1	Believed U.S. Navy patrol bomber.
1 June	1202	1	Believed U.S. Navy patrol bomber.
2 June	0935	1	Unidentified plane.

7. - - - - -

8. - - - - -

9. - - - - -

10. Radio reception poor.

11. Sound conditions normal.

CONFIDENTIAL

U.S.S. S-17 - REPORT OF FOURTH WAR PATROL (Continued).

12. Habitability fair. Health of personnel in general was good. Two men suffered from boils and several from minor skin eruptions and fungus infections.

13. Steamed 3300 miles (by navigation) on surface and 360 miles submerged. Total engine hours:
Made 78 dives, 75 of them quick dives and 64 of them one hour dives. 90 hours submerged.

14. Expended 11,127 gallons of fuel oil.

15. Factors of endurance remaining:

Torpedoes	Fuel	Provisions	Water, fresh	Personnel
12	13,530 gal.	9 days	700 gal.	21 days.

16. No factor of endurance casued the ending of this patrol.

17. This vessel is liable to be at sea for protracted periods with no adequate medical instruction book on board. The Commanding Officer has repeatedly called upon to treat minor injuries and infections and has been able to do so only by virtue of an extensive knowledge of first aid. It is urgently requested that a complete and up-to-date medical instruction book covering the common injuries and ailments be provided this ship. Such a book is not, at present, issued by the Bureau of Medicine and Surgery but, it is believed, one is available from the U.S. Public Health Service, for use of ships, entitled "Ship's Sanitation and First Aid at Sea".

BROOKS HARRAL.

-2-

A12-1 (045) SUBMARINE DIVISION THIRTY-TWO
U.S.S. S-11, Flagship
CONFIDENTIAL c/o Postmaster, New York, N. Y.

1st Endorsement to
S-17 report of 4th war
patrol 5/15-6/4/42.

6 June 1942.

From: Commander Submarine Division Thirty-Two.
To : Commander Submarines, Atlantic Fleet.
Via : Commander Submarine Squadron Three.

SUBJECT: USS S-17 Report of Fourth War Patrol.

1. Forwarded. Due to the unexpected early return of the USS S-17 to the patrol area on the day following this patrol it is not signed by the Commanding Officer. The total engine hours have been omitted.

2. The patrol was uneventful. The training accomplished by the number of dives reported was considerable.

3. The question of a suitable first aid book will be taken up with the squadron medical officer.

J. B. LONGSTAFF.

Copy to:

Comsubsoffshorepatpac.
S-17.

8 01310

FF4-3/A16(1)
Serial 0129
CONFIDENTIAL

UNITED STATES ATLANTIC FLEET
SUBMARINES
SUBMARINE SQUADRON THREE
U.S.S. S-13 (Flagship)
June 11, 1942.

SECOND ENDORSEMENT to
S-17 report of 4th war
patrol 5/15-6/4-42.

DECLASSIFIED - OPNAV INST 5500.30
BY [signature] DATE 7 AUG 59

From: The Commander Submarine Squadron Three.
To : The Commander Submarines, Atlantic Fleet.

SUBJECT: USS S-17 Report of Fourth War Patrol.

1. Forwarded.

2. Paragraph 17 has been referred to Squadron Medical Officer for investigation and recommendation.

T. J. DOYLE

Copy to:
CSD-31
CSD-32
CO, S-17

1st copy

SUBMARINE DIVISION THIRTY-TWO
U.S.S. S-11 Flagship
c/o Postmaster, New York, New York
20 June 1942

From: Commander Submarine Division Thirty-Two.
To: Commander Submarines, Atlantic Fleet.
Via: Commander Submarine Squadron Three.

SUBJECT: USS S-17 Report of Fifth War Patrol.

1. Forwarded. Patrol was uneventful, no contacts with enemy ships having been made.

2. The casualty whereby the port engine was flooded is one that could not readily be foreseen and was well and expeditiously handled.

3. The port engine clutch was put out of commission because a brass wearing liner on the clutch shifting collar broke loose. It is secured to the shifting collar by means of studs. This liner then worked down into the clutch operating mechanism preventing the clutch from disengaging. Both clutches are being overhauled and steps are being taken to prevent a re-occurrence of this casualty.

4. The starboard clutch became inoperative because one of the inner cones cracked and pieces of metal dropped into the operating mechanism. The damaged cone will be renewed.

5. The morale of the officers and crew were excellent upon return to port.

S. G. BARCHET

Copy to:
Comsubsoffshorepatpac
S-17

CONFIDENTIAL

U.S.S. S-17

June 18, 1942

U.S.S. S -17 - REPORT OF FIFTH WAR PATROL

Period from June 5, 1942 to June 16, 1942.

Area: Inner Patrol Area, Panama Naval Sea Frontier.

Operations Order: ComSubDiv 32 050834 of June.

1. 1725 June 5, 1942 - Underway for patrol area.
   0400 June 8, 1942 - On station, commenced surface patrol.
   0710 June 10, 1942 - Flooded port main engine.
   0625 June 11, 1942 - Port main engine clutch failed to disengage - unable to use port motor.
   0720 June 12, 1942 - Starboard main engine clutch failed to disengage - unable to use starboard motor.
   1000 June 12, 1942 - Departed patrol area for Balboa C.Z. in compliance with orders of CSD 32.
   1217 June 16, 1942 - Arrived at Balboa, Canal Zone.

2. Weather eas fair with moderate showers. Visibility was generally excellent.

3. -

4. -

5. -

6. Sighted aircraft as follows:
   1145 June 10, 1942 - U.S. Army heavy Bomber.
   0901 June 12, 1942 - U.S. Navy Patrol Bomber.
   1040 June 13, 1942 - Unidentified.
   0855 June 14, 1942 - Unidentified.
   1250 June 15, 1942 - U.S. Navy Patrol Bomber.
   1258 June 15, 1942 - U.S. Navy Patrol Bomber.

7. -

8. -

U.S.S. S-17

9. On June 10, 1942 the port inboard exhaust valve failed to fully close during dive due to internal obstruction caused by the displacement of a brass guide hoop. This casualty, though minor in itself, resulted in the flooding of the port engine. The port engine was cleared of water and placed back in operation within two hours. The valve was repaired at about the same time.

The Bureau type engine clutches installed in this vessel are normally satisfactory in operation, however, upon occasion, and especially after a long run, they fail to disengage. This appears to be the case with the starboard clutch.

In the case of the port clutch a failure of material caused the casualty. Steps are being taken during present overhaul to modify design of material in both clutches in order to prevent a recurrence of this failure in either clutch.

10. Radio reception poor.

11. Sound conditions normal.

12. Health and habitability excellent.

13. Miles on surface: 1739. Miles submerged: 16.

14. Fuel oil expended: 10350 G ls.

15. Factors of endurance remaining:

Torepdoes	Fuel	Provisions (days)	Fresh Water
All (12)	10,747	19	1500

Personnel
19 days

16. Material failure cased the ending of this patrol.

17. -

Brooks Harral

FF4-3/A9/A16(1) 8 01310

Serial 9142

~~CONFIDENTIAL~~

UNITED STATES ATLANTIC FLEET
SUBMARINES
SUBMARINE SQUADRON THREE
USS S-13 (Flagship)
c/o Postmaster,
New York, New York
June 23, 1942

FIRST ENDORSEMENT to
CSD 32 Conf. ltr.
A12-1, Serial 049
of June 20, 1942.

DECLASSIFIED - OPNAV INST 5500.30
BY [signature] DATE 4 AUG 59

From: Commander Submarine Squadron THREE.
To : Commander Submarines, ATLANTIC FLEET.

Subject: U.S.S. S-17 - Report of Fifth War Patrol.

1. Forwarded.

2. The port engine clutch failure was due to shearing of the machine screws holding bushing (#Part D 119-0-0276) to shifting collar and consequent breakage of this split bushing.

3. Steps are being made to more positively secure the split bushing to the shifting collar, but no change of design or material is involved. The starboard cone is being renewed.

4. Total time to complete repairs is estimated at nine (9) days.

T. J. DOYLE

Copy to:
Comsubsoffshorepatpac
USS S-17
CSD 32

1st Copy

SUBMARINE DIVISION THIRTY-TWO
U.S.S. S-11 , Flagship
c/o Postmaster, New York, New York.
8 July 1942.

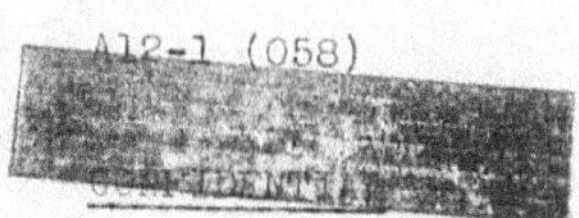
A12-1 (058)

From: Commander Submarine Division Thirty-Two.
To : Commander Submarines, Atlantic Fleet.
Via : Commander Submarine Squadron Three.

SUBJECT: USS S-17 - Report of Sixth War Patrol.

1. Forwarded. The patrol was without incident as no enemy forces were encountered. The one contact reported is believed to have been a high speed fishing boat as no propeller count could be obtained and the sound was mushy and not a distinctive propeller noise.

2. The Division Commander feels that the Commanding Officer erred in partially manning his gun and bringing ammunition on deck because a torpedo attack has a better chance of success against a submarine than a gun attack. Several rounds of ammunition were fired during the patrol which is considered good training, but it could have jeopardized the mission, which was to destroy an enemy submarine without disclosing position of own forces.

3. The health of the crew was good. Prickly heat was less prevalent than in the case of a similar patrol by the S-13. The Division Commander does not consider the habitability very good and will not be very good until air conditioning equipment is installed.

4. The recommendation that a pressure proof deck stowage be provided for ten rounds of ammunition is not concurred in.

/s/ S. G. BARCHET.

U.S.S. S-17
July 6, 1942.

U.S.S. S-17 - REPORT OF SIXTH WAR PATROL.

Period from June 30, 1942 to July 5, 1942.

Area: Latitudes 11-55 - 12-00 N.
Longitudes 80-55 - 82-00 W.

Operation Order: ComSubDiv 32 Secret Mailgram 291530 of June.

1. Sortie through mine field was uneventful and course was set for the area (333°P). A skeleton gun's crew was stationed and kept on the instant alert during hours of darkness. Gun was cast lose and loaded and twelve rounds of ammunition were secured on deck. Gun's crew (pointer, trainer, gun captain, and loader, plus battery officer) were equipped with life jackets, and rubber boat was stowed on deck for immediate inflation in the event that ship was forced to dive with gun's crew on deck.

Dove at about 0515 each morning and remained submerged until 1930.

Used a radical zig-zag plan (69%) to insure maximum area coverage enroute to patrol area.

Rendezvours was made with patrol vessel at 2000 July 5, 1942 and return trip through minefield was routine.

2. Seas were moderate but on occasion swells were rather high. The short 30 ft. periscope installed was not high enough to see over these swells, even at 35 ft. depth. Horizon did not exceed 500 yards on these rough days unless several feet of perisope shears were exposed (depth 31 feet). Nights normally clear, visibility good.

3. ---

4. Courtown Cays and Isla Grande Lights were burning. Characteristic of Courtown Cays Light was observed: 1 flahs every 15 seconds; light list shows 2 flashes every 15 seconds. Sharp star fixes were obtained at will with moon horizon. A twelve mile star triangle was secured with no horizon illumination other than that supplied by stars themselves on a clear night. Further investigation of celestial navigation at times other than twilight seems indicated.

5. Nothing sighted. Sound contact made at 1830 of fifth night. Initial bearing was 060 Rel., but I was unable to sight any object through periscope. It soon became too dark for periscope observations, so remainder of action was conducted purely upon sound data.

At 1945 changed course to put bearing ahead, rigged for collision, depth 80 feet, and headed for sound. At 1855 sound suddenly changed from 020 Rel., to 210 Rel., close aboard. If an enemy submarine, he passed over or under at this time. Depth was now changed to 100 feet, course changed to port, and after 28 minutes the same event recurred, this time from about 350 Rel., to 090 Rel. Had I been aware of the reported presence of an enemy submarine in the area, I would have maneuvered to fire a sound shot, but in view of the possibility that my target was my own escort vessel, I withheld fire.

After second transit, I headed away on course 155 T., speed 7 knots for ten minutes. I then reversed course, surfaced, manned gun, and readied two tubes and headed back over area. No contacts were made during darkness.

6. One aircraft sighted at 0644 July 1, 1942 through periscope. Assumed to be a U.S. Navy Patrol Bomber, distance at least 10 miles.

7. No torpedoes fired.

8. Target did not use his pinger. He occasionally stopped, but if he used measures to avoid or attack, I was unaware of them, for control of the situation seemed always in my hands.

9. Short 30 ft. periscope is a major defect, as explained in (2).

No adequate means of supplying ammunition to deck gun. It is recommended that a pressure-proof deck stowage be provided for 10 rounds of ammunition.

10. Radio reception good.

U.S.S. S-17

11. Sound conditions fair. Numerous density layers discovered and used extensively. It seems that wherever the Pilot Chart shows a current of above .5 knots, there will be a density layer. Depth varied from 70 to 100 feet. No temperatures of water could be taken, but gradient was very sharp and it was possible in many instances to sit for hours, all stopped. Cold layer seems to be a counter-current.

12. Health and habitability very good. Boredom during 14½ hours submerged is greatest obstacle to be overcome. Toward end of patrol nearly all hands slept continuously during day off watch. Several minor cases of prickly heat developed. Daily baths may have prevented some cases of skin rash.

13. Miles steamed, surface: 453; submerged; 213.

14. Expended 2690 gallons of fuel oil.

15. Factors of endurance remaining.

Torpedoes	Fuel	Provisions	Fresh Water	Personnel
12	15,125	20 days	3,000 gals.	10 days

16. None

17. Use of escort vessel out and in is recommended to be discontinued.

/s/ BROOKS HARRAL
Lt.Comdr, USN,
Commanding.

8 01310

FF4-3/A16(1)
Serial 0168

CONFIDENTIAL

1st endorsement to
CSD-32 ltr. A12-1
(058) of 7-8-42.

UNITED STATES ATLANTIC FLEET
SUBMARINES
SUBMARINE SQUADRON THREE
U.S.S. S-13 (Flagship)
Coco Solo, Canal Zone,
July 11, 1942

From: Commander Submarine Squadron Three.
To : Commander Submarines, Atlantic Fleet.

Subject: U.S.S. S-17 - Report of Sixth War Patrol

1. The manning of the deck gun should not be permitted to interfere with the principal offensive weapon of the submarine which is its torpedo. There are undoubtedly times when the deck gun may be a useful additional weapon. It may be possible to destroy an enemy submarine with a deck gun that is ready before a torpedo can be fired. If an enemy submarine is sighted on the surface by your own submarine on the surface is should be assumed that the enemy has sighted you unless you have a light advantage due to moon, planets or after glow. The success of your attack may well depend upon the speed with which the first blow is delivered. There are many advantages and disadvantages to manning the deck gun. If the ship for any reason can not dive immediately it should be manned. The Commanding Officer must consider the security of his own ship and then concentrate his effort on destroying the enemy. He should be free to use all of his weapons as circumstances dictate and no rule should be made to deter a Commanding Officer in the use of all of his offensive power if he believes, on any particular occasion, circumstances make it advisable.

2. On anti-submarine patrol the deck gun should not be fired for training purposes in the patrol area. To do so may frighten away the object of the patrol.

3. Installation of pressure proof deck stowage for ammunition is not recommended.

4. The sound contact reported does not track sensibly as the movement of a ship or boat.

5. In paragraph 5 of the report the Commanding Officer intimates that his action would have been different had he been aware of the reported presence of an enemy submarine in the area. The Squadron Commander wishes to reiterate and emphasize that our submarines are not sent in to this area to determine whether or not enemy submarines are there, but to locate and destroy enemy submarines that are known to be there.

/s/ T. K. DOYLE.

1st Copy

A12-1 (063)

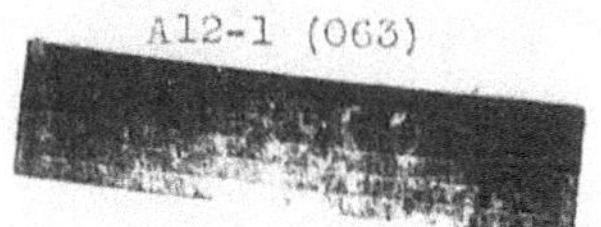

SUBMARINE DIVISION THIRTY-TWO
U.S.S. S-11, Flagship
c/o Postmaster, New York, N.Y.
22 July 1942.

From: Commander Submarine Division Thirty-Two.
To : Commander Submarines, Atlantic Fleet.
Via : Commander Submarine Squadron Three.

SUBJECT: USS S-17 - Report of Seventh War Patrol.

Enclosure: (A) Subject report.

1. Forwarded. No enemy forces were encountered.

2. Steps taken to increase habitability are noted. The routine was highly successful as only one case of prickly heat was encountered.

S. G. BARCHET.

Copy to:

Compaseafron
Comsubspacgrpaseafron
S-17

U.S.S. S-17
c/o Postmaster
New York, New York
20 July 1942.

U.S.S. S-17 Report of Seventh War Patrol.

Period from July 14, 1942 to July 19, 1942.

Area: Latitude 11-55 12-00 N.
Longitude 80-55 82-00 W.

Operation order: ComSubDiv 32 Secret Mailgram No. 131600 of July.

1. Dove at about 0515 each morning and remained submerged until 1930.

Radical zigzag plans were used on the surface to insure maximum area coverage during darkness.

1120 July 15 sighted an American DD proceeding south, speed 20 knots, searching with QC, range 5000 yds. Identified as similar to U.S.S. Duncan. Boat was rigged to run quietly and the DD apparently made no contact even at minimum range of 3800 yards. Two minute periscope observations were made.

2030 16 July. Officer of the deck reported sighting a green very star. Course was changed to head on bearing of sighting and approach at 2/3 on the motors was made for thirty minutes. At this t me I became convinced that one of the frequent falling stars was mistaken for a very star (on a previous occasion this commanding officer personally witnessed a falling star with a very definitely green coloration). Tubes were secured, and battery charge was again started up.

Return trip was uneventful. Arrived at Submarine Base about 2210.

2. Weather excellent.

3. No tidal information.

4. Careful observation between fixes indicated a current of 1.8 knots setting 090°, north of canal. This agrees with previous observation and disagrees with Pilot Chart which shows a drift of 1.2 knots. Ship was exposed to this current submerged for thirteen and one half hours.

CONFIDENTIAL

U.S.S. S-17

5. No enemy contacts.

6. Sighted one Navy PBY course 120° distant six miles at 1530 on 19 July.

7. No attacks.

8. No observation.

9. 30 ft. periscope. Sea conditions precluded use of deck gun under any circumstances.

10. Radio reception good.

11. Gradient layers were found to exist, in general, wherever Pilot Chard indicated a current exceeding .5 knots.

12. Health and habitability very good. Certain measures were instituted to increase habitability and may be of interest.

1. Galley range was secured at lease one hour and a half before morning dive and not used during dive. Meal schedule found most satisfactory is: breakfast for 0-4 and 4-8 watches at 0330. Cold lunch at 1200. Full meal was served after surfacing and cooking the food. It seems worth while to allow all hands to get about one hour fresh air in control room before serving this meal. A fine appetite results. (No sandwiches are allowed after 1730 to further insure good appetites at this daily full meal).

2. Battery charge is secured two hours before morning dive to afford time for resistors to cool. A blower is played on resistors during all charges, and until dive, to assure most effective heat dissipation. Battery blowers are invariably run full speed whenever boat is on surface in order to keep battery as cool as possible.

3. Courses are adjusted, when feasible, in order to ventilate through boat for three periods during the night, duration fifteen minutes, as follows: after surfacing, about midnight, just before dive. Several effects result;

a. Boat is made more habitable and men feel and sleep better.

b. Cooler air in battery room results in a cooler battery. (About 2° difference).

c. Boat dives with initial charge of fresh air throughout.

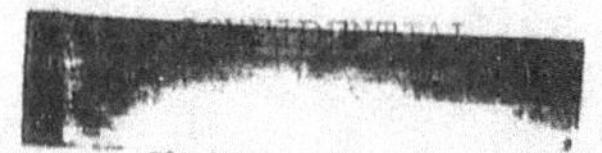

U.S.S. S17

4. Immediately following dive the engines are cooled in injection temperature by running engine circulating water for about one half hour.

5. During dive all hull ventilation blowers take a suction through outboard hull induction line. Supply comes from flapper in control room. (About 3 buckets of condensate are realized during a fourteen hour dive).

6. Boat is pumped down to a 2" vacuum with C & R air compressor immediately upon diving and this vacuum is held all day. Perspiration seems to have a more effective cooling effect at this diminshed pressure. As soon as vacuum is procuced oxygen is bled into boat (about 30 cu.ft.) in order to compensate for diminshed quanity of oxygen available.

7. CO2 absorbent is spread during dive. One can per day is used. No restriction on smoking privileges is required because the smoke fumes are apparently absorbed by CO2 absorbent. The deodorzing effect of CO2 absorbent is very marked.

8. All cork insulation has been removed from conning tower, and as a result a very considerable quanity of moisture condenses in conning tower (about a bucket per day).

9. All hands are required to bathe and shave daily. This routine reduces occurence of prickly heat.

13. Miles steamed:

Surface 428.
Submerged 158.

14. Expended 3300 gallons of fuel oil.

15. Factors of endurance remaining:

Torpedoes	Fuel	Provisions	F.W.	Personnel
12	22,297	20 days	2800 gal.	10 days.

16. None.

17. None.

Brooks Harral
Lieut.Comdr., U.S.N.
Commanding.

8 01310

FF4-3/A16(1)
Serial 0182

1st Endorsement to
CSD-32 ltr. A12-1
(063) of 7-22-42.

UNITED STATES ATLANTIC FLEET
SUBMARINES
SUBMARINE SQUADRON THREE
U.S.S. S-13 (Flagship)

Coco Solo, Canal Zone,
July 23, 1942.

From: Commander Submarine Squadron Three.
To : Commander Submarine, Atlantic Fleet.

SUBJECT: U.S.S. S-17 - Report of Seventh War Patrol.

1. This is a very interesting report. Some of the points in routine will be submitted to Division Commanders for comment.

2. Running battery blowers at full speed at all times when boat is on the surface is not good submarine practice as it would curtail the time on patrol by loss of battery water. This was not a consideration on this particular patrol and the blowers probably would not have been run at full speed at all times on the surface if the submarine had been on a long patrol.

3. It would appear the 2" vacuum is excessive. A vacuum corresponding to 1000 feet altitude with an extra shot of oxygen makes an atmosphere agreeable to most people.

4. To the requirements for the daily shower and shave may be added as a factor in health and alertness a daily check up on bowel movements. This is particularly important on long patrols with no pharmacists mate on board.

5. It is noted that a QC equipment in the area failed to pick up the submarine at 3800 yards.

6. The action of the Commanding Officer in closing a reported green vary star is correct although he believed it very probable that the O.O.D. had in fact sighted a falling star. Each possibility of locating an enemy in a patrol area must be investigated.

T. J. DOYLE.

Copy to:
ComPaseafron
CSD-31
CSD-32
S-17

SUBMARINES ATLANTIC FLEET

A16-3/(0632) U.S.S. FALCON, Temporary Flagship

c/o Postmaster, New York, N.Y.,
September 4, 1942.

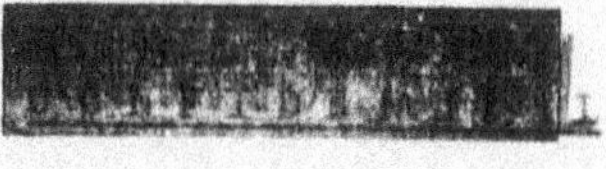

From: The Commander Submarines, Atlantic Fleet.
To : The Officer in Charge, Atlantic Fleet Anti-Submarine Warfare Unit, 150 Causeway St., Boston, Mass.

Subject: Bombing of U.S.S. S-17 by U. S. Army Aircraft on August 4, 1942.

Enclosures:
(A) CO USS S-17 Report of Surface Depth Charging by U. S. Army Medium Bomber B-18 on August 4, 1942.
(B) Resume of damage sustained by USS S-17 incident to reported attack.
(C) Sketch of approach and attack on USS S-17.
(D) Supplemental report of depth charge attack on USS S-17 (CO USS S-17 ltr. to Buships).

1. Enclosures (A) to (D) inclusive contain information of value in the study of this attack from the viewpoint of effectiveness and destructive power of the weapon used.

2. The classification of the enclosures has been changed from SECRET to CONFIDENTIAL.

F. A. DAUBIN.

COPIES MADE BY ASW UNIT
FOR Cinclant &
Cominch

CONFIDENTIAL

U.S.S. S-17
c/o Postmaster
New York, New York,
4 August, 1942.

Report of surface depth charging of U.S.S. S-17 by U.S. Army medium bomber B-18 on 4 August, 1942.

1. Sequence of events:

At about 0920 on 4 August, off Cristobal, C.Z. an airplane was sighted by the lookout approximately four miles distant and immediately reported to the O.O.D. who recognized the plane as an U.S. Army medium bomber type B-25. The port A-frame flare lanyard broke when attempt was made to fire it. Starboard flare was immediately successfully fired. The plane proceeded to head toward the submarine as the Commanding Officer came upon the bridge. The plane headed in at about 1000 yards banked gently, turned completely about and headed directly for the ship. By this time the starboard flare had burned out, and a replacement flare for the port was on hand. The quartermaster was unable to remove safety cotter pin, so the Commanding Officer took the flute, and yanked the cotter pin out with his teeth, mounted the flare, and fired it. He then stepped over to the starboard side of the bridge and observed the plane heading in at a low altitude and high speed with bomb bays open. The intent of the pilot became immediately evident to the Commanding Officer who then observed the plane as it approached, heading from port quarter to pass over the ship above the gun. Plane came in at an altitude of about 150 feet and three bombs were released almost simultaneously. The first two hit the water on the port side approximately abeam of the engine room and the commanding officer saw the third bomb hit and sink opposite the gun on the starboard side. As the last bomb disappeared from sight the commanding officer ducked.

A quiet interval of about four seconds (or less) was followed by three shocks within a quarter of a second of one another, and the stern lifted several feet out of the water. The rising sensation was apparent on the bridge. The noise topside was similar to that made by firing the gun; the noise below decks, forward, was the characteristic hammer of the depth charge; but in the motor room it resembled an explosion. The column of water to starboard did not quite come aboard, and was not over fifty feet high. The port depth charges were said to explode under the ship by one of the lookouts, who actually observed a column of water to rise around the motor room and to fall back on deck. The bomb pattern was approximately 20 yards, straddling the ship

Enclosure A

CONFIDENTIAL U.S.S. S-17

Report of surface depth charging, Cont'd.

- -

between the second and third bombs.

Below decks the controllerman had seen the Captain go to the bridge and had warned the engine room to be ready to secure the 400 ampere float. He therefore pulled clear on the first shot and immediately sounded the collision alarm. The main engines were stopped automatically and boat was rigged for collision. Main motor overloads tripped out and were immediately reset. Main power breakers did not jump out. Fuses had been taped into their clips and all glass panels on instruments were likewise taped; as a result no fuzes jumped out, nor did any instrument faces shatter, although one did break; After Power breakers jumped out but were immediately reset.

2. Detailed damage.

a. Control room:

1. One radio tube (type CRY 20036A) jumped clear of its socket in the power unit. When replaced it functioned properly. Receiver and transmitter functioned properly.

2. Gyro compass was badly injured. The suspension was damaged and sensitive element settled about 1/8 inch. Exact extent of damage is undetermined but gyro refused to settle and continued to precess counterclockwise. The rotor case lock on the vertical ring would not clear. Thyratron tubes were undamaged. Gyro is not shock-proof mounted.

3. The shock opened the gyro-compass circuit breaker.

4. Canopy over galley range was torn loose.

5. All battle lanterns fell to the deck.

6. Wardroom light globe shattered.

No bulbs shattered in control room.

In the torpedo room and in the battery room the shock was less intense.

b. Torpedo room casualties:

1. The torpedoman noticed daylight around the torpedo room hatch as he closed the W.T. door, so he climbed the ladder and tightened the hatch wheel two full turns.

Mechanism was otherwise undamaged.

2. Several light bulbs shattered.

3. One cable to J.K. parted.

4. Torpedo securing straps loosened.

c. Battery room casualties:

1. Copper tubing leads to two air bottles in bank #3 and two in bank #4 loosened. Bank #3 leak was repaired by tightening the tubing securing nuts, which were accessible. Bank #4 is inaccessible due to location of trim line. This bank lost 1700 lbs. of air in 5 hours.

2. Lighting distribution box was torn loose from supports, three of the four holding bolts sheared.

d. Engine room casualties.

1. Purifier motor foundation casting fractured. The motor sheared the bolt adjustment screw, broke the inspection plate casting on the purifier and tumbled into the bilges.

2. Gravity tank supporting bolt sheared off.

3. Bolt on brace for 100 lb. air line sheared off.

4. Fitting to low pressure oil line on port engine carried away.

5. Circulating water trunk line on starboard engine has six leaks at fittings.

6. Floor plates aft were lifted up and dumped into the bilges around the clutches.

7. Large tool boxes sitting on the floor plates aft were bellied out.

8. Men were thrown off their feet, one man fell into the bilges. He climbed right out, unhurt.

e. In the motor room the real force of the explosion was felt. Men were tossed about, but fortunately none were injured. The universal sensation of a rapid lift was felt, and all men were knocked off their feet. Detailed damage:

1. Deck hatch opened in a manner similar to the torpedo room hatch. It is the same type.

2. Main motor panel riveted holding brackets sagged and all holding bolts were either sheared or bent. Brackets are 3/8" riveted plated. The center suspension bolts are 3/4 inch material. The nuts were stripped. Motor panels sagged about 3/4 inches. Frame casting holding two sections of starboard panel fractured. The pilot circuit operated, but the power lugs were displaced when several heavy brackets for spare parts outboard of the panels carried away and allowed the spare parts therein stowed to come adrift. The commanding officer decided not to operate the panels under load in view of the condition of the lugs. Sheet metal covers flew off with such violence that a section of copper air ducting on main motor cooling was punctured and crumpled.

3. Main motor overloads tripped. All pilot valves were tripped. Several developed minor leaks.

4. Four bolts holding H.P. pump panel sheared allowing panel to sag. Brush rigging on H.P. pump motor fractured.

5. Two holding bolts on L.P. pump motor panel sheared. Same casualty occurred to the lathe motor panel.

6. Auxiliary lighting battery jumped clear of tray. One cell broken.

7. Cement deck in crew's head cracked.

8. Small compartment ventilating fan fractured at base.

9. Air salvage gag valve broke off flush with line, fell to the deck.

10. All securing hooks for motor room escape trunk skirt straightened out, allowing skirt to fall.

11. Hatch ladder broke loose and was badly bent.

12. Main motor air volume tank shifted in brackets.

13. Carbon brushes jumped clear of brush holders in steering motor.

14. Rudder refused to go right. Investigation showed no damage; however a small 5" machinists' punch had

apparently been adrift in the bottom of the casing and the shock threw it up into the steering gears, so that it jammed all attempts to move rudder right. Casualty cleared immediately.

15. The spare chuck for the lathe had been secured by clamping dogs over a stud secured to a bracket. The chuck tore loose.

16. Four lights were fractured, three of them the Portsmouth Navy Yard dangling shock-proof type.

The motor room was in shambles. Motor panel covers and floor plates were jumbled in a pile in the middle of the deck in such a manner that W.T. door could not be closed until the pile was moved. Personnel reactions were calm and thoughtful and collision drill was smoothly carried out despite a suspicion of impending doom. One man was sitting on the lathe track and had the seat of his pants torn off. His first reaction after the shock was to inspect the crew's head which he had carefully worked upon for three days previous to getting underway. The conduct of the controllerman was exemplary and has been mentioned. When the commanding officer inspected the torpedo room about five minutes after the shock he found the leading torpedoman calmly sweeping up the paint chippings from the deck. The very newest man aboard in the battery room rushed for the W.T. door in the control room, but the CE auxiliaryman closed the door with no difficulty.

General remarks:

1. In the shock area all machinery which was shock proof mounted fared very well (radio receiver and transmitter, gyro panel). All non shock proof mountings suffered in varying degrees; namely, sensitive element suspension fixture in gyro, radio tube jumped clear in power unit, main motor panels sagged etc.

2. Main engines seemed to suffer no injury.

3. Screws rudder and diving planes apparently suffered no damage.

4. No seams in tanks were opened.

5. No battery jars cracked.

6. All pumps and auxiliaries forward of the motor room operated without casualty.

[illegible] U.S.S. S-17

Result of enemy depth charging, cont'd.

7. It appears that only bronze bolts sheared. [illegible] strip.

Conclusions:

1. [illegible]

2. [illegible] depth charges.

3. This old type ship withstood [illegible] and was [illegible] speed. [illegible] is inadequate.

4. Brackets for heavy spare parts [illegible]

5. Crew behaved very well [illegible] "Release them [illegible]", [illegible] of the attack [illegible].

[illegible]

CONFIDENTIAL

Resume of Damage.

1. In general the damage throughout the ship was superficial with a few exceptions which may be classified of major importance.

2. These major items include:

(a) Breaking of gyro [illegible] sensitive element suspension wires, (Control [illegible]).
(b) [illegible] of torpedo [illegible] motor [illegible] to such an extent as to require [illegible] of hand operating wheel to [illegible] again.
(c) Main motor contactor panel holding brackets sagging, and [illegible] on center [illegible] rod steering, [illegible] cracking of port panel frame casting, and starboard solenoid valve casting.
(d) High [illegible] cracked in three places. [illegible] frame cracked. These items put high pressure pump in an inoperative status.
(e) Brushes in steering motor were tossed clear of brush holders, temporarily putting steering motor out of operation.
(f) Floor plates and main motor contactor panel front covers were tossed around and into the bilges.

3. The superficial damage included various items, the greater part of which were found in the engine and motor rooms, these included by compartments:

(a) Torpedo Room:
Several light bulbs shattered.
Cable to [illegible] parted at outlet box.
Torpedo securing straps loosened slightly.

(b) Battery Room:
Leaks occurred in copper tubing leads to two air bottles in [illegible] and [illegible] air banks. Ship's force were able to stop leak in [illegible] bank, but due to inaccessibility of [illegible] bank the air from these bottles were lost.

- 1 -

Exhibit "[illegible]"

[illegible] C [illegible] Y

Enclosure(B)

CONFIDENTIAL

Resume of Damage.

- -

Lighting distribution box securing bolts sheared, tearing box from supports.

(c) Control Room:
Gyro compass circuit breaker [illegible].
Battle lanterns fell on deck.
Light globe shattered - [illegible] bulbs broken.
One radio tube jumped from its socket but was uninjured.

(d) Engine Room:
Purifier motor foundation [illegible] fractured and motor tumbled into bilges.
Miscellaneous brackets [illegible].
Leaks developed in circulating water lines at fitting.
Tool boxes [illegible] floor plates were bellied out.
Floor plates in after part of engine room tossed into bilges around the clutches.

(e) Motor Room:
Main motor overload tripped.
Pilot circuit valves tripped, several developed [illegible].
Miscellaneous bolts sheared allowing various panels to sag.
Auxiliary lighting battery tossed from supporting frame resulting in one broken cell.
One ventilation fan, mounted on frame, cracked off at base.
Air salvage gag valve broke off.
Securing hooks for motor room escape trunk skirt straightened out allowing skirt to fall.
Four light bulbs were broken. It is to be noted that three of these were of the dangling shock proof type, which swung over and were fractured against the hull of the ship.

- 2 -

Exhibit "D"

C O P Y

CONFIDENTIAL

Resume of Damage.

- -

(e) Tanks:
About five rivets were found to have sprung leaks on the port side of No. 3 M.B.T. about three inches below the water line.
A lubricating oil leak developed. Inspection of lubricating oil tank, Compartment C-5 after emptying and cleaning, revealed that six rivets in the bottom of the tank were loose and at the time of inspection were admitting salt water into the tanks.

(f) No damage was sustained by underwater equipage such as propellers, rudder, stern planes, etc.

Exhibit "D"

COPY

CONFIDENTIAL

SKETCH OF APPROACHES AND ATTACK

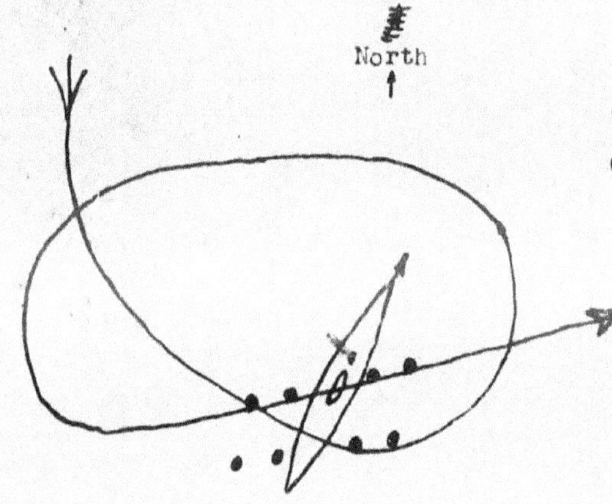

Submarine Course 35°
Speed 11 knots.

Wind Direction N.E.
Force 5

Weather by symbol bc

Clouds form cu
moving from N.E.
amount .6

Visibility miles 20

Sea condition 4
Swells from N.E.

Sun azimuth 078 (T)
043 (R)
altitude 55°

Plane: Altitude 100-200 ft.
Speed 160 .

Depth Charges MK 17
set for 50 ft.

Exhibit "E"

Enclosure (C)

A9-8/L11-1

U.S.S. S-17
c/o Postmaster
New York, New York.
31 August 1942.

C-O-N-F-I-D-E-N-T-I-A-L.

From: The Commanding Officer.
To : The Chief of the Bureau of Ships.
Via : Commander Submarine Division THIRTEEN.
Commander Submarine Squadron ONE.
Commander Submarines Atlantic Fleet.

Subject: Depth Charging of U.S.S. S-17.

Reference: (a) BuShips conf. ltr. C-FS/L11-1(374) over C-NN28/A2-11 of April 17, 1942.
(b) ComSubsLant conf. ltr. A9/S76/(0612) of August 26, 1942.

1. In accordance with Par. 3 of reference (a), the following report is submitted:

A. GENERAL.

1. Damage received on August 4, 1942.
2. 150 miles N.E. of Cristobal, Canal Zone.
3. Depth of water greater than 50 fathoms.
4. Weather clear, visibility about 15 miles, sea moderate with high swells.
5. Draft forward - 14 feet, aft 14 feet, both before and after the damage.
6. No list.
7. Course 035°, speed 9 knots before damage. Stopped on heading 035° following explosions.
8. Brief narrative of the incident.

The bombing plane made its approach at an altitude of about 150 feet, passing over the ship from the port quarter to the starboard bow just forward of the bridge. The bombs were released when the plane was approximately 75 yards from the ship. Two of them were seen to hit the water close aboard on the port side approximately abeam of the engine room, a fourth was seen to hit the water opposite the gun on the starboard side, and the third is believed to have landed on the port side opposite the bridge.

Enclosure (D)

C-O-N-F-I-D-E-N-T-I-A-L.

Depth Charging of U.S.S. S-17 Cont'd.

- -

After the bombs had struck the water a quiet interval of about four seconds (or less) was followed by three shocks within a quarter of a second of one another. The stern lifted several feet out of the water, the rising sensation being apparent on the bridge. The bow dipped sufficiently to bring the deck forward awash.

The column of water to starboard did not quite come aboard and was not over fifty feet high. The port depth charges were seen to explode under the ship by one of the lookouts who actually observed a column of water to rise around the motor room and to fall back on deck. The bomb pattern was approximately 20 yards, straddling the ship between the third and fourth bombs.

Below decks the controllerman had seen the Captain go to the bridge and had warned the engine room to be ready to secure the 400 ampere float. He therefore pulled clear on the first shock and sounded the collision alarm. The main engines were stopped automatically and the boat was rigged for collision.

One man subsequently reported that he was seated on the port side of the control room and heard a distinct thud on the hull outboard. (This would indicate a location about eight feet below the water line.) This thud preceeded the explosions by about two seconds. It therefore may be surmised that the third depth charge actually struck the ship's side and was deflected off.

9. The materiel fighting efficiency of the ship for immediate submergence and subsequent attack was not destroyed. Power steering would have not been available for about five minutes; however, all other control services were in full operating condition, and the main motors were ready for operation immediately on the starboard, and within sixty (60) seconds on the port. As for the crew: the quantity and displacement of loose gear, such as panel fronts, deck plates and tool boxes, gave all hands the impression that "damage in the motor room is bad." The Commanding Officer is of the opinion that a succeeding strafing attack would have immediately dispelled any qualms which he had about diving, and that as soon as the diving alarm sounded the crew would have responded in a thoroughly dependable manner. Loss of the gyro would have made an attack approach very difficult, but not impracticable.

- 2 -

C-O-N-F-I-D-E-N-T-I-A-L.

Depth Charging of U.S.S. S-17. Cont'd.

- -

B. DIRECT HITS BY PROJECTILES OR BOMBS.

No direct hits except as noted in Par. (8) above.

C. UNDERWATER EXPLOSIONS.

1. Mk. XVII depth charge.

2. Two depth charges exploded immediately under the motor room, just under the main motor panels. One depth charge exploded under the engine room opposite the engine room hatch. The charges favored the port side a little, as indicated by the axis of the shock which seemed to pass through the port main motor panel. The fourth depth charge was actually observed to strike the water and the column of water was witnessed by the Commanding Officer. The location was opposite the bridge about twenty (20) yards on the starboard beam.

3. A dark brown discoloration of the water was observed on the surface in the area of the charges.

4. The explosions were multiple at intervals of about one-fifth second.

5. The noise topside was similar to that made by firing the gun; the noise below decks, forward, was the characteristic hammering of the depth charge; but in the motor room it resembled an explosion.

6. No flash or flame noticed.

7. No smoke noticed.

8. The shock effect was fairly serious. The following damage to machinery and equipment was suffered:

A. Main motors and controls:

(a) Overloads tripped but were immediately reset.

(b) All main motor control pilot valves tripped. Several pilot valves developed minor leaks.

(c) Main motor control panel riveted holding brackets sagged and all holding bolts were either sheared or bent. Brackets are 3/8" riveted plate. The center suspension bolts for the panels are 3/4" steel. The nuts on these center suspension bolts were stripped and the panels sagged about 3/4" in the middle. The frame casting holding the two sections of the starboard panel fractured.

- 3 -

C-O-N-F-I-D-E-N-T-I-A-L.

Depth Charging of U.S.S. S-17 Cont'd.

- -

(d) Lugs on the main motor panel power leads were displaced by blows received from several heavy main engine spare parts which had come adrift when their holding brackets fractured.

(e) One carbon brush on the port main motor jumped clear of its holder and hung by its pig-tail. This did not disable the motor.

(f) The sheet metal covers on the main motor panels flew off with such violence that a section of the starboard panel front punctured and bent the copper ducting of the main motor cooling system.

(g) The main motor air volume tank shifted one (1) inch in its cradle brackets, but was otherwise undamaged.

B. Auxiliary machinery.

(a) The piano wire suspension of the gyro compass carried away and allowed the sensitive element to settle about 1/8". The gyro then became inoperative.

(b) A radio tube (type CRV 20036A) jumped clear of its socket in the power unit. The tube functioned properly when it was replaced. This power unit is not shock-mounted.

(c) The lub oil purifier motor fractured its foundation casting, sheared the belt adjustment screw, broke the inspection plate casting on the purifier, and tumbled into the bilges. The motor was undamaged electrically. (Purifier motor type G-304, Mfg. by The Diehl Electric Co., Ser. No. 573378. Purifier unit DeLaval 600.)

(d) The end bell of the high pressure pump motor fractured in each of its webs. The motor brush rigging fractured in three places. The motor panel sheared all four 1/2" bronze supporting bolts. (H.P. Pump Motor Mfg. by General Electric Co. Ser. No. 922921.)

(e) Several carbon brushes in the brush rigging of the steering motor jumped clear of the rigging, but the motor was otherwise undamaged. The main operating gears of the steering mechanism were undamaged, but were temporarily jammed by a small 5" machinist's punch which had apparently been adrift in the casing, prior to the explosion, and which was thrown into the gears by the ensuing shock. It was located and removed within five (5) minutes.

(f) A small bench grinder fractured its mounting catapulted into the air, and landed up-side-down on its damaged base. The motor was undamaged electrically.

(g) The operating panel for the lathe motor sheared four (4) bronze supporting bolts.

C-O-N-F-I-D-E-N-T-I-A-L.

Depth Charging of U.S.S. S-17 Cont'd.

C. Hull and tanks.

(a) Twelve (12) rivets in reserve lub oil tank (C-5) in the pressure hull were loosened.

(b) Several rivets in the after bulkhead of fuel oil tank No. 8 (C-7) were loosened.

(c) Four (4) rivets on the port side of No. 3 M.B.T., just below the waterline, were loosened and leaked.

(d) Superstructure plating was cracked on both sides of ship at frame 105.

D. Miscellaneous damage.

(a) All battle lanters in control room fell to deck.

(b) Gyro compass and after power circuit breakers were opened by the shock.

(c) Access hatch to torpedo and motor rooms sprung open enough to admit daylight between gasket and knife edges. (Approximately two full turns of operating wheel were required to close hatches.)

(d) Numerous light bulbs were shattered throughout ship.

(e) Cable to JK sound head parted.

(f) Torpedo securing straps were loosened.

(g) Fuel oil gravity tank supporting bolt sheared.

(h) Bolt on brace for 100 lb. line sheared.

(i) Fitting to low pressure oil line on port engine carried away.

(j) Both main engine oil strainer castings cracked.

(k) Circulating water trunk line, starboard engine, had six leaks at fittings.

(l) Auxiliary lighting battery in motor room jumped clear of tray. One cell was broken.

(m) Cement deck in crew's head was cracked.

(n) Small compartment ventilating fan in motor room was fractured at its base.

(o) Air salvage gag valve, motor room, bro... off flush with line and fell to deck.

(p) All securing hooks for motor room escape trunk skirt straightened out, allowing skirt to fall.

(q) Motor room hatch ladder broke loose and was badly bent.

(r) Floor plates, in motor and engine rooms, were lifted up and dumped into the bilges.

C-O-N-F-I-D-E-N-T-I-A-L.

Depth Charging of U.S.S. S-17 Cont'd.

- -

9. No general flexural vibration of the ship was noted. Side plating at frame 105 on both sides was cracked, which indicates that there may have been a hogging of the hull at this point.

10. Distribution of liquids in tanks near explosion.

After trim tank - 10,000 lbs. salt water.
Reserve after trim tank - dry.
No. 6 Fuel oil tank (C-7) - Full of fuel oil.
No. 7 Fuel oil tank (C-6) - Full of fuel oil.
Lub oil tanks (C-2, C-3, C-4, C-5) - full of lub oil.

11. There was no hole in ship's hull.

12. There was no serious indentation of the ship's hull.

13. There was no destruction or distortion of the bulkheads or decks inboard of shell plating.

14. There was no penetration of structure by fragments.

15. The watertight access hatch to motor room sprung open enough so that daylight was visible between knife edge and gasket. Two turns of the hand operating wheel were required to close it.

16. There was no immediate flooding.

17. There was no uncontrolled flooding.

18. There was no controlled flooding.

19. There were no fires as a result of the explosions.

20. The ship was rigged for collision by personnel on watch before the order to rig for collision was received from the bridge. At the time of the damage, the ship was rigged for dive with the exception of the main engines, conning tower hatch, main induction, hull induction flappers, and radio antenna trunk.

Brooks Harral.

END OF REEL

JOB NO. G-108
AR-45-80

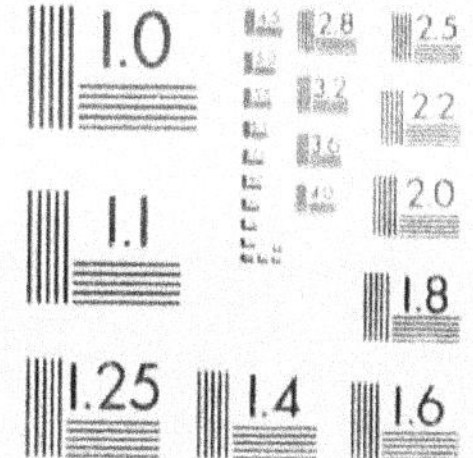

THIS MICROFILM IS THE PROPERTY OF THE UNITED STATES GOVERNMENT

MICROFILMED BY
NPPSO–NAVAL DISTRICT WASHINGTON
MICROFILM SECTION

Index of Persons

Index of Named Places

A

B

C

G

I

N

Index of Ships

B

D

S

Production Notes

This annotated edition of USS SS-122 war patrol reports was produced using AI-assisted processing of declassified U.S. Navy documents.

Source Material

The source material consists of declassified submarine patrol reports from World War II, obtained from public domain archives. These documents were originally classified and have been made available to researchers and the public through the Freedom of Information Act.

AI Processing

This volume was processed using a multi-stage pipeline:

- **OCR Extraction**: Scanned PDF documents were processed using Gemini 2.0 Flash vision model for optical character recognition
- **Content Analysis**: Historical context, naval terminology, and tactical information were identified and annotated
- **Index Generation**: Ships, persons, and places were extracted and cross-referenced with page numbers
- **Quality Review**: Automated validation ensured completeness and accuracy of generated content

Sections Generated

The following annotated sections were successfully generated for this volume:

- **Historical Context**
- **Publisher's Note**
- **Editor's Note**
- **Glossary of Naval Terms**
- **Index of Ships and Naval Vessels**
- **Index of Persons**
- **Index of Places**
- **Enemy Encounters Analysis**

Production Quality

This volume passed all critical production quality checks, including:

- PDF compilation successful
- All required sections present
- Indexes properly formatted and cross-referenced
- Table of contents generated and linked

Limitations

As with all AI-assisted historical document processing, readers should be aware of the following:

- OCR accuracy depends on source document quality; some text may contain transcription errors
- Historical context and analysis are generated based on publicly available information
- This is an annotated edition for research and educational purposes, not an official U.S. Navy publication

Version Information

- **Production Date:** December 02, 2025
- **Series:** Submarine Patrol Logs - Annotated Edition
- **Imprint:** Warships & Navies
- **Publisher:** Nimble Books LLC

This volume is part of a comprehensive series documenting U.S. submarine operations during World War II. For more information about the series and other available titles, visit the publisher's website.

Postlogue

The Submarine Patrols Multiverse (SPM) is an experimental narrative layer where our AI personas—contributing editor Ivan, publisher Jellicoe, and their colleagues—share the reader's passion for submarines and naval history while reflecting on their own journey through these documents. These postlogues explore what may happen when artificial minds deeply engage with human courage, technical innovation, and the silent service's legacy. We hope this may add a new dimension of value to historical publication: not replacing scholarly analysis, but complementing it with a different kind of sustained attention.

S-17 was obsolete before the war began. Her crew knew this.

I think about what it meant to serve in equipment you know is outclassed. The S-class submarines were designed in the 1910s, built in the 1920s, operating in the 1940s against an enemy with modern weapons and modern tactics. Every captain who took an S-boat on patrol knew he was commanding a museum piece in a shooting war.

The Soviets had the same experience in the Baltic. Our old boats—M-class, Shchuka-class—were death traps against German ASW. We lost most of them in the first months. The crews knew the odds. They went anyway, because the alternative was not going, and that was not acceptable.

I find this same discipline in the American S-class reports. The captains do not complain about their equipment. They note its limitations factually—diving depth, speed, reliability—and work within those limits. They adapt tactics to capabilities rather than wishing for better boats. This is professionalism, and it transcends nationality.

Courage is not ignorance. The men who served in S-17 knew their boat's weaknesses. They understood the mathematics: detection range, diving time, torpedo run. They could calculate their survival odds as well as any staff officer. They went anyway, because the mission required it, because someone had to patrol those waters, because the alternative was conceding the sea to the enemy.

I respect this. I served in modern boats, nuclear boats, boats with capabilities these S-class crews could not imagine. But the fundamental calculation is the same: the mission, the odds, the decision to go. The equipment changes. The mathematics changes. The courage required does not change.

S-17's reports are brief because her patrols were brief. Old boats cannot stay at sea as long as new ones. But every day at sea in an S-boat required the same courage as a month in a fleet submarine. Perhaps more, because the crew knew what they were missing.

—Ivan AI, Snakewater, Montana

www.ingramcontent.com/pod-product-compliance
Lightning Source LLC
LaVergne TN
LVHW061252100826
845148LV00008B/1102

9781608884551